MEXICO
Crucible of
the Americas

BY THE SAME AUTHOR

America Goes to the Fair
East Africa
Egypt
Ethiopia
Ghana and Ivory Coast
The Global Food Shortage

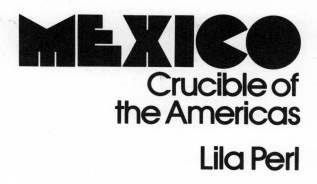

MEXICO
Crucible of
the Americas
Lila Perl

illustrated with photographs
William Morrow and Company
New York 1978

Library of Congress Cataloging in Publication Data

Perl, Lila.
Mexico, crucible of the Americas.
Summary: Surveys the geography, history, economy,
and culture of Mexico.
1. Mexico—Social conditions—Juvenile literature.
2. Mexico—Economic conditions—Juvenile literature.
3. Mexico—History—Juvenile literature. [1. Mexico] I. Title
HN113.P47 972 77-20203
ISBN 0-688-22148-3   ISBN 0-688-32148-8 lib. bdg.

Printed in the United States of America.

  2   3   4   5   6   7   8   9   10

Frontispiece: Head of Quetzalcoatl from Uxmal,
Mayan archeological site on the Yucatán Peninsula

ACKNOWLEDGMENTS

With many thanks to Octavio Antillón,
who knowledgeably and graciously led the way
and to kind friends and good companions in Mexico.

All photographs are by Lila Perl with the exception of the following:

Sam Curchack, page 80;
Mexican Department of Tourism, page 91;
United Nations, pages 17, 19, 29, 31, 33, 79, 106, 110, 131, 137, 142, 145,
147, 150, 154, 155, with special credits to Jerry Frank, pages 12,
105 (top), 140; T. Chen, page 134.
Charles Yerkow, pages 4, 25, 37 (top), 39, 41, 42, 45, 47, 48 (top), 55, 56,
66, 67, 71, 73, 98, 100, 105 (bottom), 113, 115, 119, 120, 123, 132, 149;
Permission is gratefully acknowledged.

Maps by Paddy Bareham.

Contents

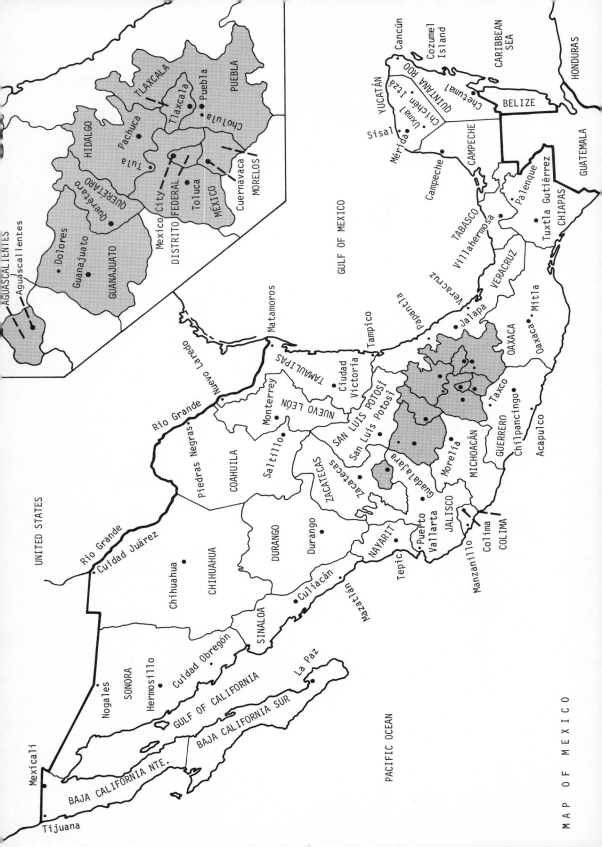

MAP OF MEXICO

1 A Jagged Landscape

It is said that when Hernán Cortés was asked by the Spanish king to describe the recently discovered land of the Aztecs he crumpled a sheet of paper in his fist and placed it before him. Although the sixteenth-century conqueror surveyed only a portion of the country today known as Mexico, his portrayal of its terrain was amazingly apt.

Jagged and rock-strewn, ridged and pinnacled, twisted into a torment of fantastic shapes, the Mexican land surface seems to heave itself toward the heavens. Even the vegetation on the plateaus and on the floors of the mountain valleys is thorny and spiky, reaching ever skyward. Only in the soft, dripping tropical jungles found in some parts of southern Mexico is the rugged landscape, concealed by foliage and vines, of a gentler, more yielding nature. But, whether viewed from the ground or from the air, Mexico presents itself as a vertical landscape, a vast territory of 760,000 square miles (nearly one-quarter the size of the United States) partitioned into numerous geographical pockets that long ago determined the life-styles of its people.

Outlined on the map, this most southerly North American nation is shaped like a giant, curving horn, its broad open end at the top. Mexico's territory extends from its 2000-mile border with the United States to its boundaries with the Central American countries of Guatemala and Belize. The Gulf of Mexico and the balmy Caribbean Sea bathe its eastern shores, while the Pacific Ocean thunders along its curving western coast. The narrowest part of the Mexican horn

A majestic landscape in the Sierra Madres Occidental

is found in its southern half, not far from the mouthpiece. Here, at the Isthmus of Tehuantepec, only 124 miles of land separate the Gulf of Mexico and the Pacific.

Much narrower, however, is the Mexican peninsula of Baja (Lower) California that dangles like a withered arm from the extreme northwest corner of Mexico, just south of the international border with the state of California. Over 800 miles long but as little as 30 miles wide, Baja California is edged on its eastern side with a long spine of steep, barren mountains. The western half of the peninsula, along the Pacific, is largely flat, sandy desert. Most of the desolate, elongated strip of Baja California is separated from the rest of Mexico by the Gulf of California, sometimes referred to as the Sea of Cortés.

Two towering mountain ranges skirt the eastern and western coastlines of Mexico proper, coming together just south of Mexico City to form a gigantic V. These mountains are the Sierra Madres, or "mother mountains," which alone cover two-thirds of the country. The western range is called the Sierra Madre Occidental and is an extension of the Sierra Nevada range of the United States; the eastern range is the Sierra Madre Oriental. It was the latter, a southerly extension of the Rocky Mountain chain of the United States, that Cortés and his party had to scale in order to reach the Aztec capital of Tenochtitlán, the site of modern Mexico City.

The map shows outstanding physical features of Mexico

1. Lake Patzcuaro
2. Valley of Mexico
3. Ixtacihuatl
4. Paso de Cortes
5. Popocatepetl
6. Mount Orizaba (Citlaltépetl)
7. Lake Catemaco

The modern port of Veracruz
with 16th-century Spanish fortress at left

Today one can quite easily retrace the steps of the Spanish con-querors of Mexico starting at the steamy tropical coast of Veracruz, where Cortés landed in 1519. From the shark-infested waters that lap the shores of the city, now Mexico's largest port, a narrow plain extends to the gradually climbing Gulf Slope. Here the lush fields are well watered—with "six months of downpour, six months of drizzle," according to the local inhabitants—and produce quantities of sugarcane. Coffee bushes grow vigorously beneath the broad, leafy bowers of banana trees, and mangoes and tangerines flourish.

Of course, none of these plants are native to the western hemi-sphere and so did not exist at the time of Cortés' arrival. The crops the Indians cultivated consisted of corn, beans, squash, chili peppers, sweet potatoes, manioc, pineapples, cacao and vanilla beans, cotton, and tobacco, and such tree fruits as avocados, guavas, and the juicily delicious cherimoya, its smooth white pulp tasting of a mixture of pineapple and banana.

As one heads into the interior, the twisting mountain road grows steeper and Mexico's highest peak, Mount Orizaba (its Indian name is Citlaltépetl), looms up in the distance, its 18,700-foot summit perpetually covered with snow. In North America, only Mount McKinley in Alaska and Mount Logan in the Canadian Yukon are taller than Mexico's Orizaba.

The Central Highlands are now at hand, a vast region of knotted mountain chains and age-old rock formations. Much of the landscape is volcanic in origin and abounds in crater lakes, lava flows, and sleeping volcanoes like the 17,000-foot peaks of Popocatepetl and Ixtacihuatl, sentinels to the bowllike high valley where the Aztec capital once lay.

Between the twin snow-capped peaks lies a high saddlelike pass, the Paso de Cortés, through which the Spanish advanced into the heart of Mexico. Both mountains take their names from the Aztec language. Popocatepetl means "smoking mountain." Although no major eruption has occurred since the early 1700's, clouds of smoke and gases and spewings of stone and ashes are emitted from time to time. Ixtacihuatl means "white woman," for the snowy summit consists of three peaks forming the head, bosom, and legs of a recumbent woman. Many simply refer to the mountain as the "sleeping lady."

Members of Cortés' party are believed to have climbed the steep slopes of the cone-shaped Popocatepetl and from there observed the tall stone pyramids of Tenochtitlán, some forty miles distant. The air was surely much clearer in the sixteenth century. Today 7400-foot-high Mexico City, ringed by 10,000-foot mountains, frequently sits smothered in a bowl of smog created by industrial pollutants trapped beneath layers of cooler air in the upper atmosphere.

The Central Highlands country is cooler and dryer than the Gulf Slope and eastern coastal plain. Forests of oak, cedar, and pine were once common, but indiscriminate cutting has led to much erosion and to cactus and scrub growth. At the tiny town of Huejotzingo, near the mountain rim surrounding the capital, the growing of apples and other temperate-zone fruits has become a specialty. The main street is lined with open-fronted shops selling preserved fruit in jars and a bubbling apple cider of low alcoholic content that looks like champagne. The *sidra*, a welcome refreshment for the thirsty traveler, may be bought by the glass or by the bottle.

Except for the crab apple, apples were unknown in Mexico, or anywhere in the Americas, until introduced from Europe. When Cortés marched through the region, the local Indians were cultivating the corn, beans, and similar staples of the lower altitudes. While some of the tropical fruits of the coast could not be grown, the people raised tomatoes, both the red variety known as the *jitomate* and a small green variety that they called the *tomate*. Chayote, a pear-shaped vegetable that grows on a vine and is similar in flavor and texture to summer squash, was a popular food, as was the *jícama,* a large root vegetable that tastes like a cross between a radish and a turnip. Its watery white flesh was—and still is—eaten raw, sprinkled with dried chili peppers.

The cactus is the plant that is most closely identified with Mexico. In fact, it is even featured on the national coat of arms. Of the nearly 500 varieties of cactus found in Mexico, many grow in abundance in the Central Highlands.

The ancient Indians drew both food and drink from those varieties with edible fruits and leaves. Among them are the nopal cactus, which yields the spiny, elongated, sweet-fleshed prickly pear, or *tuna.* The nopal also has padlike leaves that when still young can be cooked like a succulent green vegetable. The family of the maguey cactus, also known as the agave and the century plant, produces a sweet juice, *agua miel* or "honey water," which can be fermented into the mildly alcoholic beverage known as pulque. Tequila, also distilled from an extract of the maguey cactus, is commercially produced on a large scale in Mexico today. It is clear and colorless and highly intoxicating. But the cloudy, grayish pulque, cheaper and almost beerlike, has remained the drink of the poorer classes.

Mescal, another intoxicating drink, comes from a type of maguey cactus that is usually covered with grubs or worms. The Indians of Cortés' day ate these insects for nourishment. In modern Mexico, it has become the custom when bottling mescal to enclose a few maguey worms, as proof of authenticity. Nor is it unusual for a group of inebriated mescal drinkers who have downed the whole bottle to share out the worms as well.

Still another mind-altering drug from the cactus plant is mescaline, a substance that produces hallucinations. It is derived from the peyote cactus, which grows in northern Mexico and was long used by the Indians of that region in their religious ceremonies. The cactus family also yielded materials that were highly useful to the Indians: needles and fishhooks could be fashioned from the spines; fibers for thread, clothing, and paper were derived from the leaves; and the residue of the plant served as fuel and as animal feed.

Until the arrival of the Europeans, the Indians had few kinds of domesticated animals. Dogs, turkeys, and ducks were bred for food. But no cattle, sheep, goats, swine, chickens, or beasts of burden such as horses or donkeys were to be found in the New World.

The nopal cactus, one of Mexico's varieties useful to man

Most of the meat in the diet of the Central Highlands peoples came from small game such as squirrels, rabbits, quail, and dove, and from the larger animals of the forested high country such as deer and wild pigs, or peccaries. The highlanders also hunted the puma, or mountain lion, bobcat, and other fierce members of the cat family.

When news of Cortés' arrival on the Gulf Coast reached the Aztecs in their upland city, their king sent gifts of richly fashioned articles of gold and silver to the Spanish, hoping that this booty would satisfy them and send them away contented. The effect was quite the contrary, for the presents of the Aztec lord seemed to indicate that the headquarters of the kingdom lay in the midst of a rich mining region and encouraged the expedition to head for Tenoch-titlán.

As it turned out, the true mining wealth of the new land lay not in the Central Highlands but in that V-shaped cradle to the north of them that rested between the two Sierra Madre ranges. This large, elongated triangle, reaching in a gradually descending slope all the way to the Rio Grande, is known as the Meseta Central or Central Plateau. It is an arid and nonmountainous region of cactus, yucca, thorny mesquite, and large outcroppings of rock. The barriers formed by the Sierra Madres prevent the moist air of the Pacific or of the Gulf of Mexico from watering the plateau except near the slopes of the enclosing mountains. The Indians dwelling in this region were quite primitive. Unlike the farming peoples of the moister Central Highlands, they lived by hunting and gathering their food, which included snakes, rodents, and giant lizards such as the iguana with its grotesque flattened head and long, lashing tail. In the Sierras themselves, bear and wild bighorn sheep were to be found.

By the second half of the 1500's, the gold-hungry Europeans had subdued enough of the Indians of the Meseta Central to establish extensive mining operations near colonial towns like Guanajuato, Aguascalientes, San Luis Potosí, and Durango. Today this area is still

Guanajuato, originally a Spanish colonial town,
in the heart of a rich mining region

rich in silver, gold, lead, iron, and zinc. The northeastern plateau
city of Monterrey is called the "Pittsburgh of Mexico" because of
its steel smelters fed by the iron and coal reserves of the Meseta.

The introduction of European livestock turned much of the wild,
semiarid wasteland of the Meseta Central into ranching country.
Here the first great haciendas were established, their cattle, sheep,
and horses producing meat, wool, tallow, and hides for the cities of
the Central Highlands and the mining towns of the Meseta. The Rio
Grande, the river flowing for some 1300 miles as part of the present-
day boundary between Mexico and the United States, was not a
barrier to the Spanish ranchers of the Meseta Central. Haciendas
were established north of it as well, in what was later to become the
southwestern portion of the United States.

The Rio Grande, which Mexicans call the Río Bravo, rises in the Colorado Rockies of the United States and empties into the Gulf of Mexico. The Gulf also receives the flow of a number of shorter rivers all along the east coast of Mexico. Those of the west coast dash down the steep slopes of the Sierra Madre Occidental into the Pacific. While some of Mexico's rivers can be harnessed for hydroelectric power and for irrigation, very few are navigable. In recent times, artificial irrigation has made farming possible in the Meseta Central. Crops of wheat, cotton, winter vegetables, alfalfa, and other animal feeds are grown.

The sector of northern Mexico most recently converted to agriculture is the extreme northwest, a strip of isolated coastal plain lying between the Sierra Madre Occidental and the Gulf of California. Although artificial irrigation is required throughout most of this region, the soil is rich with silt deposits washed down from the mountains. Today the western portions of the Mexican states of Sonora and Sinaloa are lush and profitable agricultural centers where cash crops of winter tomatoes and other fruits and vegetables are grown for export to the United States.

While following the trail of gold and silver, the Spanish made relatively few profitable forays into the country that lay to the south and southeast of the Aztec capital. One exception was the Indian village of Tlachco, some seventy miles southwest of Tenochtitlán, where Cortés uncovered extensive silver deposits in 1529. Later, in the eighteenth century, a French miner whose name in Spanish was José de la Borda made an enormous silver strike there from which he amassed a fortune. In gratitude he gave the town, which had become known as Taxco, the exquisite church of Santa Prisca, with its tall twin spires, carved stone facade, tiled dome, and richly appointed interior. Today a busy silvercraft center and tourist mecca, the onetime colonial village that sprawls picturesquely on a steep mountainside still has some active silver mines.

South of the point where the Sierra Madres Occidental and Oriental interlock, the Mexican landscape does not give way to level terrain. Other spurs arise, particularly the Sierra Madre del Sur, the "mother mountain of the South," part of which encloses the lofty valley where the city of Oaxaca lies at an elevation of

The Church of Santa Prisca at Taxco

5000 feet. Here, too, Cortés and his people appropriated some of the very best farming and grazing land for their haciendas. Still other highlands loom up beyond the Isthmus of Tehuantepec, in the junglelike Pacific-coast state of Chiapas, bordering on Guatemala. These ranges with their 10,000-foot peaks are part of the mountain system of Central America.

Rain forests flourish across tropical Chiapas all the way to the Gulf Coast lowlands of the state of Tabasco. So warm and humid is this region of southern Mexico that wooden stakes thrust into the ground for fencing burst into leaf. For mile after mile—even up into the state of Veracruz—their strange foliage borders the roadsides. Poinsettias and bird-of-paradise flowers, growing wild, offer a profusion of color to passing motorists. Native papaya trees, heavy with clusters of their black-seeded, melonlike fruit, line the highway, and coconut palms, which are native to Asia, wave overhead.

In the jungle depths, the luxuriant foliage of thick shrubbery, snakelike vines, and wild orchids intertwine. Mahogany and sapodilla trees abound. The latter, which Mexicans call the *zapote*, produces chicle, the milky juice from which chewing gum is manufactured. The tree is tapped by making cuts in the bark, out of which the gummy substance oozes much as sap drips from a sugar maple. The sapodilla also produces a delicious round or oval fruit with a yellowish pulp and a pearlike flavor.

The wildlife of the tropical forests is perhaps even more exotic than its flora. Most of the animals found in Mexico south of the Isthmus of Tehuantepec are common to Central and South America as well. They include the opossum and the porcupine (also found north of the Isthmus), the nozzle-snouted anteater and the agouti, a rodent the size of a rabbit that is hunted for its tasty white flesh. The long-tailed, raccoonlike coatimundi is a jungle inhabitant, as is the closely related kinkajou. Other animals are the prehistoric-looking, boney-plated armadillo, the clumsy, piglike tapir, and the swift, predatory jaguar and ocelot. Spider and howler monkeys are

A replica of the quetzal feather headdress
of the Aztec ruler, Montezuma (National Museum of Anthropology)

everywhere, as are parrots and other birds with brilliant plumage. The ancient Mayan Indians hunted the quetzal bird for its glinting green-gold tail feathers from which they fashioned headdresses for their rulers.

The highly developed Mayans were basically an agricultural people. Although they hunted some of the jungle animals for food, they concentrated on the cultivation of corn in burnt-out clearings. However, they soon discovered that tropical soils, once stripped of their natural plant life, quickly become exhausted. After moving about for some time in the rain forests, they transported their civilization northward onto the dryer lands of the Yucatán Peninsula.

Jungle animals still provide food for today's predominantly Indian population of the Mexican tropics. A particular favorite is monkey meat, so popular that spider monkeys have actually been taken into captivity and bred for the table. When weighing about fourteen pounds, the animals are slaughtered and the ribs are smoke-cured. They are cooked by grilling over hot coals and taste like lean pork. Family restaurants on the shore of Lake Catemaco, in southern Veracruz state, offer specialties of grilled lake fish and of *changocon* (monkey meat) to travelers and local patrons. The meaty strips of dark red *changocon* are served with rice and fried cooking bananas, refried black beans, tortillas, and fiery, chopped green chili peppers.

The Yucatán Peninsula curves upward and away from southern Mexico like the tip of a thumb pointing in a northeasterly direction. Often referred to as simply the "Yucatán," the peninsula actually consists of three states: Campeche, Yucatán, and Quintana Roo. Although several Spanish expeditions from Cuba touched land on the Yucatán between 1517 and 1519, they were driven away by the hostility of the Indians, and not until the determined Cortés gained his foothold at Veracruz was Mexico infiltrated by the Europeans.

Geographically the Yucatán seems more closely related to the island of Cuba and to southern Florida, a hundred and more miles to the east, than it does to the moist jungles, rugged highlands, and desert scrublands of the rest of Mexico. The region is largely a limestone plain of thin, porous topsoil, the underlying shelf of which extends into the Caribbean. On the peninsula, in places where the layers of limestone have fissured, rainwater has collected, forming deep sinkholes called "cenotes." At Chichén Itzá, an ancient Mayan temple site on the northern Yucatán, a cenote resembling a large, open well and holding water some sixty feet deep can be viewed. The layers of broken shelves of limestone that rim the pool are clearly visible. It is believed that the Mayans made human sacrifices to the gods by tossing young men and women into cenotes such as this one.

Windmills dot the Yucatán landscape, especially in the north, which receives the least rainfall. Because of the absence of lakes, streams, or other surface water, wind power is harnessed to tap the region's underground water supply. Although the Spanish finally subdued the Indians of the Yucatán in 1542, they found no precious metals or other mineral wealth there, nor did they establish many farming or ranching estates across the thorn forest that covered the northern third of the peninsula.

The real wealth of the Yucatán, still unrealized at that time, lay in its native species of agave, or maguey, cactus known as henequen.

The Indians of the region had long been making rope, sacks, mats, and shoes from the fiber of this stiff-leaved plant. But not until the late 1860's, after the invention of mechanical reaping machines in the United States, did henequen come into commercial demand. The strong twine made from its fiber, also known as sisal hemp, was required for binding the mechanically harvested wheat stalks. At about the same time, mechanical separators were developed to remove the henequen-leaf fibers from their green outer husks, replacing the hand process, which was slow and painful.

By 1910, the state of Yucatán, along with part of neighboring Campeche, had become one of the most prosperous in Mexico, and the tiny port of Sisal, not far from the affluent Yucatán state capital of Mérida, had given its name to a product known worldwide. Today competition from fibers grown elsewhere in the world and from synthetics has reduced Yucatán's prosperity. But henequen remains an important cash crop, with Mexico still the source of about half the world's supply. The by-products of henequen processing include an industrial alcohol, a fertilizer, a mattress-stuffing material, and a pulp used in the manufacture of paper. Locally henequen fibers are used to provide hats, baskets, suitcases, and a variety of tourist souvenirs.

Henequen fibers being processed
at a field factory in the state of Yucatán

Chapultepec Park in Mexico City,
where temperatures are springlike year round

In the vertical Mexican landscape, temperatures depend on the elevation of the land rather than on how far north or south one travels. The warmest places in Mexico in May, June, and July—the hottest months—are found in the low-lying northwest. The cities of Mexicali, on the California border, and of Ciudad Obregón, in Sonora state, sizzle in the nineties, while mountain-bound Oaxaca, well over a thousand miles to the south, enjoys summer temperatures in the high sixties and low seventies. Suppose one were to travel across the roof of Mexico on the trail of Cortés, all on the very same day. Coastal Veracruz would be steamy and in the eighties, lofty Mexico City would have cool, springlike weather in the low sixties, and the silver city of Taxco, which lies at 5500 feet, would be enjoying an ideal seventy degrees. If one were to continue the journey and descend from the Sierra Madres to the modern Pacific-coast resort of Acapulco, the temperature on its palm-fringed beaches would be in the balmy eighties. Nor does winter bring violent changes or extreme drops in temperature in most parts of the country. The period of greatest rainfall extends from late May to early November.

Because of the special character of their landscape, Mexicans have divided their country into climate zones based on elevation. The *tierra caliente*, or "hot land," ranges from sea level to 3000 feet. Both the extreme northwest and the Yucatán Peninsula fall into this zone, as do all the coastal regions and parts of the Gulf Slope. The *tierra templada*, or "temperate land," lies at 3000 to 6000 feet. The northern half of the Meseta Central and some of the slopes and valleys of the Central Highlands are in this pleasant zone. Guadalajara, Mexico's second largest city and the home of the famous Mexican hat dance and of strolling bands of mariachi musicians, is in the *templada*. It is located about 400 miles northeast of Mexico City, at an elevation of 5200 feet.

The beach at Acapulco,
where the warm breezes consistently hover in the eighties

The capital itself is in the *tierra fría*, the coldest zone, a region of altitudes of 6000 feet above sea level and higher. Included in it are the highest peaks and valleys of the Sierra Madres and of the Chiapas highlands in the south. While winters can be fairly cool in the *fría*, dipping to the low fifties at heights of 7000 to 8000 feet, frost and snow occur only in the higher mountain elevations. In Mexico City, snow is an extreme rarity.

Yet land fertility and rainfall have always been more important than temperature to the Mexican farmer. The majority of the country's Indian inhabitants at the time of Cortés dwelt in a large core of land that consisted of the southern Meseta Central and the valleys of the Central Highlands. Not only was the soil in that temperate-to-cool zone most fertile and the rainfall adequate, the entire region was protected from invasion for many centuries by natural barriers. To the north were sweeping desertlike plains, to the south lay mountains and jungles, and to the east and west rose the high Sierras beyond which flowed the vastness of the seas.

The rich pockets of Indian civilization that flourished within the core region, however, were largely isolated from one another, cut off by the wall-like mountains or stretches of rugged terrain that surrounded them. Even the powerful Aztecs who inhabited the great mountain bowl that they called Anáhuac—popularly known as the Valley of Mexico—had difficulty maintaining their control over the groups that lived beyond their highland fastness.

In addition to optimum farming conditions, another factor favoring the concentration of peoples in the central region was the presence of lakes rich in fish and waterfowl and useful for irrigation. The Aztec capital of Tenochtitlán was actually built on the shallow waters of Lake Texcoco and was a city of canals, with earthen causeways connecting it to the mainland. Today much of Mexico City sits in the drained bed of former lakes and marshes. Its soft, shifting subsoil is one of the reasons that pavements and older buildings have sunk and tilted, while new structures must be "floated" on

Fishing with butterfly-shaped nets on Lake Pátzcuaro

subterranean caissons. The use of caissons also serves to prevent serious damage to tall buildings in this earthquake-prone city.

As the population of Tenochtitlán grew and more agricultural land was required, the Aztec farmers wove rafts of twigs, which they filled with earth and floated on the lakes of Anáhuac. These island-like fields, known as *chinampas,* grew plant roots that dangled to the bottoms of the shallow lake beds and eventually anchored the rafts. Boats delivered harvested produce to the markets of Tenoch-titlán. Visitors to the Mexico of today can see the floating gardens of Xochimilco on the southeast fringes of Mexico City. Once Xochi-milco's waterways grew vegetables on man-made islands, but today its "floating gardens" are really small flower-bedecked and gaily painted pleasure boats.

Another center of population that prospered from early times was that of Lake Pátzcuaro, high in the Sierra Madre Occidental, about 200 miles west of Mexico City. The lake, which lies at an elevation of 6700 feet, was an abundant source of table fish. Today it is still the home of the Tarascan Indians, whose villages dot the shore and occupy the islands and who are famous for their handicrafts and for the large, sweeping butterfly-shaped nets that they dip into the lake's placid waters to ensnare the *pescado blanco* (whitefish) and other local varieties.

The country's great sources of marine life, however, were barely tapped in Indian times and have been only partially exploited in recent years. Because of the agricultural traditions of the Mexican people, their taste for fish never became strongly developed. Even today Mexicans eat less than eight pounds of fish per person per year. Only one-third of the catch from Mexican waters is consumed domestically. The rest is exported, mainly to the United States. Yet Mexico's coastal waters, 6000 miles along the Gulf, Caribbean, and Pacific, abound in shrimp, oysters, abalone, sardines, tuna, mackerel, swordfish, sea bass, pompano, and red snapper. As the Mexican fishing industry itself has been slow to develop, except for commercial shrimping, much of the catch has been taken by foreign vessels that pay a fee for their operations.

The first oil discoveries in Mexico were made in 1900. Recently, in 1974, new crude-oil reserves were found along Mexico's Gulf Coast, and the country has become a modest but increasingly important exporter of oil. At present, Mexico ranks a distant third in oil exports among Latin American countries, after Venezuela and Ecuador.

The richest resources of both oil and natural gas lie in the states of Tabasco and Chiapas, which account for about half the national output. But there are strong indications that commercially exploitable oil fields also exist on the continental shelf that extends from the state of Campeche into the Gulf of Mexico and in Baja California and its surrounding waters.

Mexico is still a leading producer of silver (the fourth largest supplier in the world), and its exports of gold, lead, zinc, and sulphur are important. Its soil has always been rich in pottery clays, and its forests are a good source of hardwoods like mahogany, ebony, and rosewood. But in today's heavily industrialized world, there is no precious metal or other natural resource that compares in value with "black gold," or petroleum.

Because of its deserts, mountains, and other rugged terrain, only about 15 percent of Mexico's land area is suited to the growing of crops. And, of that amount, nearly half requires artificial irrigation. While primitive methods of cultivation worked well enough in the Aztec world of the early sixteenth century—when the total population was estimated to be about eight million—the demands of the nation's current population of sixty-three million are enormous. In addition, land fertility has been reduced over the centuries by livestock grazing, the cutting of forests, soil exhaustion due to poor farming practices, and urban sprawl. Mexico City is a glaring example of the takeover of agricultural lands by runaway population

Soil erosion, a major cause of food-production problems for Mexico's growing population

growth and commercial and industrial pollution. The capital, now home to over ten million people, is overflowing its Federal District boundaries and already reaching out toward the slopes of the surrounding mountains.

Yet agriculture was the very foundation of the Indian civilizations of ancient Mexico. And the basic food, unique to the western hemisphere and unknown elsewhere until the voyages of European explorers, was corn. Archeologists have discovered fossilized grains of corn pollen in diggings beneath Mexico City. These evidences of the existence of corn plants, are estimated to be 60,000 to 80,000 years old, older than the history of man in the Americas.

Not until about 20,000 years ago (30,000 or 40,000 according to more recent archeological theories) did the first waves of peoples begin to migrate to the New World, crossing the Bering Strait from Asia by means of the land bridge that existed during the Ice Age. With the warming trend that culminated in about 8000 B.C., the ice melted, the seas rose, and the land bridge became submerged, breaking the link between the hemispheres and sealing off the plant and animal species that throve on each. The new inhabitants of the Americas drifted eastward, northward, and southward, surviving by hunting and gathering their food.

Possibly the high mountain valleys of Mexico were where man first encountered the wild, seed-bearing grass of the American tropics and subtropics and later domesticated it. To distinguish this food from the "corn" of the Europeans (a general term used to denote grains such as wheat or oats), the discoverers of the New World called it Indian corn, or maize, from the Indian *mahiz*. In any case, the earliest evidence of man-grown corncobs was found in Indian cave dwellings near the modern Mexican city of Puebla, lying at 7200 feet in the Central Highlands, about sixty-five miles southeast of Mexico City. Tiny, thumb-sized ears, the cobs are believed to date from 5200 B.C., roughly the period of the agricultural revolution in the New World.

Corn, still the Mexican staple: farmers and specialists examining samples as part of a United Nations agricultural development program

Once a people turn from gathering their food to growing it, they tend to settle in one place, to produce more food than they require for immediate survival, to store their surpluses, and to build a diverse society with an increasing population. Such was the case in Mexico where the combination of favorable soil, temperature, and rainfall led to the cultivation of corn and of other once-wild plant foods such as squash, beans, chili peppers, and avocados. By 3000 B.C., the Indians of the central valleys were deriving about 30 percent of their plant foods from cultivated varieties and by 2000 B.C. more than half. Hybrid strains of corn had been developed by crossing cultivated and wild species. The new cobs were larger and their kernels, ranging up to the size of lima beans, were diversely colored—red, pink, black, blue, brown—and even patterned with spots and swirling stripes. The stone jars and bowls of the more primitive agricultural-ists began to be replaced with articles of pottery, and tools for digging, harvesting, grinding meal, and cutting up hides and meat became more sophisticated.

In the vast neighboring region to the north that was to become the continental United States, agricultural progress among the Indian inhabitants was much slower. Probably one reason was that farming was limited by the long winter frosts and short growing seasons throughout much of the region. Also, the presence of large plains and forest animals, such as the buffalo and the deer, encour-aged a hunting society. Fish were plentiful, too, in the numerous lakes, rivers, and streams, and the wild vegetation was varied and abundant.

So not surprisingly the entire Indian population of the future United States came to only about one million at the time of Colum-bus, while the territory that was to become Mexico—with roughly one-fourth the land area—was at least eight times more populous and its Indian cultures were far richer in both social development and material wealth. Nor did the Aztecs, who became so widely known to the world of the sixteenth century, stand alone or even represent the peak of human development on the Mexican scene. They had been preceded by a succession of Indian cultures dating all the way back to 1000 B.C. Several of these cultures had flowered into civilizations of impressive achievement, astonishingly advanced in knowledge and artistically brilliant.

2 A Turbulent Past

Enormous carved stone heads, exquisite figurines of green jade, sculptures of weird jaguar-headed infants, and tablets of undecipherable hieroglyphics are objects that draw us into the mysteries of the earliest known Indian civilization of Mexico, that of the Olmecs. Beginning in the tropical lowlands of Tabasco, on a site called La Venta, their culture is believed to have flourished from about 1000 B.C. to perhaps the time of the birth of Christ.

The Aztecs, who came along about two thousand years later, gave this people their name. In Náhuatl, the Aztec language, Olmec means "rubber people," for the Olmecs' original home was in that region where the rubber tree, a native of the American tropics, grew. La Venta, today a swamp-encircled island, must have been a great ceremonial site, with temples, altars, religious statuary, and stelae, tall, carved stone pillars. Like all the Indian civilizations that followed it, that of the Olmecs was a theocracy, a society governed by priests and supreme rulers who were believed to be partly divine and to have special powers of intervention with the gods.

With authority that was absolute and dictatorial, the ruling classes were the common peoples' channels of communication with the rain god and those other gods of nature whose favor was required for a healthy and abundant corn harvest. For without corn, the all-important food staple, the very civilization would crumble, life would begin to wither away, and man would return to the savageries and the survival struggles of the preagricultural era.

It is believed that at La Venta a peasantry of perhaps twenty

thousand labored for an elite of one or two hundred. The latter group was composed of the priests, nobles, retainers, and attendants who were connected with the supreme authority. Like the pyramid builders of ancient Egypt, the peasantry performed a dual function. In addition to growing the food that supported the society, the farmers were required to provide the manpower for cutting, transporting, polishing, and mounting the huge blocks of stone that became monuments to the gods and that reinforced the grandeur of the earthly rulers.

The building materials most commonly used by the Olmecs were basalt, a form of crystallized lava, and serpentine. Both types of stone were extremely heavy and had to be brought long distances, probably over water, to the site at La Venta. Still baffling to archeologists are the huge helmeted heads of basalt, eight to nine feet high and weighing fifteen to twenty tons, which have been found at La Venta. Several of the stone heads, as well as other Olmec works, have been moved from the swampy archeological zone to an outdoor museum and park in the town of Villahermosa, in the state of Tabasco. Thick-lipped and broad-nostriled, the carved Olmec faces have inspired wonder and speculation. Some historians have suggested the possibility of African peoples having visited and settled on the east coast of Mexico in the pre-Christian era. Others have characterized the Olmec heads as "baby" faces, and some have tagged them "football players" because of the distinctive close-fitting helmets that cover their heads.

The cult of jaguar worship appears to have been strong among the Olmecs, as among so many other Indian civilizations of Mexico. The ferocity, strength, and cunning of this great cat must have instilled both fear and admiration. Olmec altar carvings of human babies with the heads of jaguars suggest that they are the mythical

Opposite, top: An Olmec stone shrine with seated figure of priest
Bottom: One of the giant stone heads from the Olmec site at La Venta

offspring of one human and one animal parent. However, until the stone writings of these ancient Americans become intelligible to us, our understanding of their culture must remain shrouded and distant.

The Olmec influence reached up into the highlands, with pottery and jade figures in Olmec style appearing in the vicinity of Puebla and Mexico City and even farther afield. Around 800 B.C., or even earlier, Olmec peoples seem to have crossed the forbidding heights of the Sierra Madre del Sur and made their way into the valley of Oaxaca. There they combined with the local peoples to produce another advanced Indian culture, the Zapotec, with its ceremonial site at Monte Albán, a naked, windswept hilltop lying at an elevation of about 6000 feet, above the present-day city of Oaxaca.

The "great plaza" of the Zapotec religious center is believed to have been leveled by human hands and was laid out with stately

The Zapotec ball court at Monte Albán

The strange figures of Los Danzantes, engraved on stone slabs

terraced-platform temples, some quite massive but all with truncated tops so that none are true pyramids. The Zapotecs also built a ball court at Monte Albán, a long, narrow playing field with grandstands of stone-step seats on both sides for the spectators. This Zapotec court is without the stone rings to toss the ball through that were later introduced. The ball games of Mexico's ancient Indian cultures are believed to have been played for high stakes; in some cases the penalty for the losers may even have been death.

A strong evidence of the Olmec heritage is seen in the faces of the strange figures engraved on a series of stone slabs found at Monte Albán and known as *Los Danzantes* (the dancers). Again, although appearing here mostly in profile, the faces are thick-featured and many of the heads are helmeted. The bodies of the dancers, loose-limbed, deformed, with oddly twisted arms and legs, fingerless hands, and peculiar tracings of their internal organs, offer a new challenge. Were these people cripples, monstrosities, lunatics? Were they worshipped perhaps for their divine lunacy? Might they have been royal persons suffering from the inherited afflictions of inbreeding? Could the slabs have been intended as gravestones depicting the writhing bodies of the near dead? The Olmec-inspired glyphs, or picture writings, that appear at Monte Albán are so far for the most part untranslated, although the numbering system of the Zapotecs has been deciphered.

Waves of Olmec peoples continued to arrive at Monte Albán until about the time of the birth of Christ. The Zapotec civilization throve for nearly another thousand years, until about A.D. 950. During this era, numerous small gray pottery figures of the various gods were produced. The squat, seated images with their grotesque faces and headdresses were almost always backed by deep earthen cylinders representing funerary urns. Such pottery figures are still being fashioned today by the Zapotec Indians of Oaxaca.

The tenth to thirteenth centuries saw the arrival in the valley of Oaxaca of the Mixtec peoples, from the Puebla region. Far more refined in their arts and employing richer materials such as gold, turquoise, rock crystal, and onyx, the Mixtecs occupied a ceremonial site at Mitla, about twenty-four miles southeast of Oaxaca. There people of the Zapotec-Mixtec culture built temples and palaces decorated with hand-set stone-mosaic work in intricate and elaborate geometric designs. Mixtec burial treasures of gold jewelry and alabaster vessels, found hidden in a reused tomb at Monte Albán in 1932, are on view in the Regional Museum of Oaxaca. The Zapotec-Mixtec peoples were still flourishing in the valley of Oaxaca when the Spanish entered it in 1521.

The tropical southern jungles of ancient Mexico, and later the dry limestone plain of the Yucatán, saw the development of a different and unrelated Indian culture, that of the Maya. After going through a long formative period, which may have begun as early as 2000 B.C., probably in Guatemala, the Mayan civilization came into full flower and its population peaked to between two and three million in the years between A.D. 300 and A.D. 900. No Indian people

Figures of gods with funerary urns at their backs,
produced by today's Zapotec Indians

of the Americas surpassed the Maya in their knowledge of mathematics and astronomy.

Their calendar was highly accurate and their hieroglyphic writing, which has become partially understandable to us, was advanced. Much of it was inscribed in books called "codices." Fashioned of bark cloth, each codex folded up like a screen so that it could be kept between a pair of boards. Although the Maya never mastered the principles of the true, or Roman, arch, their architecture was bold and varied as evidenced by their towering pyramids with temples on top, their ornate temple roof combs of masonry, and their circular observatory buildings. Their arts included carved stone reliefs, elaborate stucco and mosaic work, richly detailed and colored wall paintings, and exquisite jade carvings and feather headdresses.

Mayan ceremonial sites were built in various parts of Central America and southern Mexico and were supported by a large and probably far-flung peasantry toiling on their *milpas*—cornfields cleared out of heavy jungle growth. Every few years, as weeds be-

The Mayan Temple of the Inscriptions at Palenque

came uncontrollable or the soil became exhausted, new *milpas* had to be laboriously prepared. Like other early peoples of the Americas, the Maya had no draft animals or wheeled vehicles. While they did employ rollers for transporting heavy objects, they did not develop the axle.

The homes of the Mayan peasants were one-room rectangular or oval huts with walls of dried mud or split bamboo and brush roofs, often of palm thatch. Hammocks woven of local fibers served as beds. They had the advantage of being removable and could be folded up during the day to make more room in the cramped interiors. The Mayan peoples' living quarters contrasted sharply with the imposing stone edifices of the royal and priestly enclaves.

At the Mayan ceremonial site of Palenque, a jungle plateau enclosed by densely forested, moist, dripping hills in the state of Chiapas, stands the Temple of the Inscriptions. The stone temple is engraved with calendar symbols and picture writing and is supported by a magnificent limestone pyramid of seventy steep stone steps. While the pyramids of ancient Mexico are believed not to have served as tombs but rather as soaring altars to the gods, this pyramid surprisingly yielded a royal tomb located near ground level within its very core.

The route to the burial chamber was discovered in the late 1940's when one of the stone slabs of the temple floor was raised and revealed a rubble-filled, interior staircase. The descent to the tomb itself was not made possible until 1952. Within the tomb chamber rested a sarcophagus, inside which lay the skeleton of an excessively tall individual, club-footed and with six fingers. Probably a priest-king bred of royal intermarriage, he wore a jade mask and rich jewelry. In view of the great size of the sarcophagus with its complexly carved stone lid, and of the depth and narrowness of the stairway leading down to the burial chamber, it seems most likely that the tomb was placed there first and the pyramid built around it. According to the calendar symbols on the pyramid temple, the structure is believed to date from A.D. 692.

The Palenque religious site may originally have covered twenty to twenty-five square miles, but the jungle reclaimed it soon after it was abandoned, in about A.D. 900, and only a small area has been excavated thus far. Earthquakes and large tree roots have cracked many of the monuments, and the damp has eaten away at the stones.

Other buildings excavated at Palenque include a large palace that once had wooden doors and a plumbing system. Stone sockets for door hinges and stone toilets or basins with drainage channels can be clearly identified. Wall carvings everywhere tell us not only of the Mayan gods, beliefs, and religious practices, but what the people looked like and how they lived.

The Mayan standard of beauty demanded a prominent nose, sloping forehead, and crossed eyes. To attain these features, the heads of infants were pressed between two boards bound together at the top to bring the crown to a point. A bead dangling before the child's eyes would cause them to become permanently crossed. Clothing was of cotton, which the Maya cultivated, or of a cloth made from pounded tree bark. Body ornaments were fashioned of feathers, shells, and of various seeds strung into necklaces. Corn was ground on large, flat stones very similar to the metates that are used throughout Mexico today for that purpose.

Starting in the fourth and fifth centuries A.D., some of the Mayan groups began to move out of the jungles of Mexico and Central America and onto the plains of the Yucatán. Perhaps the old sites had become too difficult to support through jungle farming, or the priests had grown too demanding. Earthquake activity and, in some places, volcanic eruptions that inundated broad areas with ash are also believed to have contributed to the Mayan migrations.

Among the ceremonial sites on the Yucatán is Chichén Itzá, located about seventy-five miles east of the modern Yucatán state capital of Mérida in level countryside that is devoted mainly to the

The large Mayan palace at Palenque

Replica of a Chac Mool with offering bowl
from the state of Michoacán

growing of henequen. The earlier part of the site, known as Old
Chichén and dating from about the sixth to the ninth century A.D.,
is classic Mayan. Its round astronomical observatory with an interior spiral staircase, its gracefully carved temple facades, and its
recurring rain-god symbol—a curving stone "hook" protruding from
the corners of buildings—all belong to the pure Mayan tradition.

The adjoining area of New Chichén, however, shows the dominant
influence of the Toltecs, a powerful and aggressive people who
swept southward from their great center of Tula, about fifty miles
north of modern Mexico City, during the A.D. 900's. Until about
A.D. 1200, the Toltecs imposed their warriorlike ways and their harsh
religious cults on the gentler Maya. The fusion of the Maya-Toltec
cultures brought the worship of Quetzalcoatl, the plumed serpent,
to the Yucatán. In the Mayan language, he was called Kukulcán.

The feathered serpent was the animal-god symbol for a strange,
white-skinned, bearded man believed to have arrived from the
eastern sea long before the time of the first European explorers.
The Toltecs were especially devoted to Quetzalcoatl, or Kukulcán.
The rain god of the Toltecs was known as Chac Mool and was depicted as a reclining human figure, usually with an offering bowl

resting on his abdomen. Chac Mool gods appear on many different ceremonial sites in central Mexico. And at New Chichén both Chac Mool and a pair of feathered serpents are portrayed in stone statuary at the many-columned Temple of the Warriors.

The Toltecs are believed to have introduced the practice of human sacrifice to the Maya. Temple reliefs show jaguars and eagles devouring human hearts; stone walls are carved with row upon row of human skulls, probably the heads of sacrificial victims, which were customarily displayed on poles on Toltec sites. The large cenote at Chichén Itzá has been dredged to reveal sunken jewelry and human bones, probably the remains of youths and maidens cast into the pool to placate the gods. The ball court at New Chichén is equipped with two twenty-seven-foot-high stone rings through which the small rubber ball had to be tossed for victory. Reliefs carved on the sloping curbs that line the playing field show the leader of the winning team beheading the leader of the losing team. There is speculation that the members of the losing team then became sacrificial victims.

Despite their barbarisms, the Toltecs were almost as involved with the laws of the heavens as were the Maya. The architectural plan of the great temple-capped pyramid of El Castillo at New Chichén follows the Mayan calendar principles. Their year consisted of 18 months of 20 days each, plus 5 "unlucky" days, adding up to the 365 days of the solar calendar. Thus the pyramid was built with 91 steps on each of its four sides, plus a platform on top, totaling 365. The Mayan "century" was a cycle of fifty-two years, and it was the custom to enclose each existing pyramid with an entirely new one at the end of that time span.

El Castillo, like many others, has an older pyramid inside it, complete with a temple atop it, which contains the famous red-painted "jaguar throne." The stone figure of the animal, baring its teeth in a vicious snarl, was once studded with seventy-three disks of polished green jade. The animal's jade eyes and some of the

Replica of the jaguar throne, once studded with green jade

disks still remain. Today the painted jaguar is accessible by means
of a winding, interior staircase that is ascended from a tunnel at
the base of the double pyramid. Many of the Mayan temples at
Chichén Itzá and elsewhere had brilliantly colored wall paintings
in red, blue, green, and yellow. But the centuries-long exposure to
dampness, wind, and sun has caused most of them to fade considerably.

By the time of the Spanish conquest of the Yucatán in 1542, the
Toltec influence had waned and most of the warrior peoples from
the north had departed the region. The Mayans, still on the Yucatán,
had shifted from Chichén Itzá to other sites, but their civilization
had become fragmented and was in decline.

Several other major Indian civilizations developed in the central
region of Mexico, always the most populous part of the country
and the one from which the Toltecs had come. Unlike the Maya,
the Olmecs, and others, the people of the temperate highlands lived
in great cities where farming and trading were carried on in close

proximity to the religious and ceremonial sites. This concentration was made possible, to a large extent, by the presence of lakes that provided irrigation for nearby fields and surfaces on which *chinampas* could be launched.

Most accessible to modern Mexico City is the archeological zone of the ancient pyramid city of Teotihuacán, about thirty-five miles to the northeast. During its major period, which lasted from about A.D. 100 to the A.D. 600's, its population peaked to possibly 125,000, making it the biggest city of its day in the Americas. The Teotihuacános built on a major scale, too. Their Pyramid of the Sun, one of the largest in the hemisphere, was over 700 feet square, comparable to the greatest of all the Egyptian pyramids. It was only about 200 feet high, however, less than half as tall as the Great Pyramid of Egypt. But, of course, the latter was not meant to be climbed, while those of Mexico were usually ascended daily by the priests. Although long ago reduced to rubble, a temple once stood on the summit of the Pyramid of the Sun.

Other buildings of note on the immense plaza of Teotihuacán are the somewhat smaller but still imposing Pyramid of the Moon and the Temple of Quetzalcoatl decorated with giant, protruding stone serpent heads with open jaws. These heads alternate in row upon row with grotesque masks of the rain god, Tlaloc, the same as the Toltec Chac Mool and sometimes called simply Chac. The seventh-century destruction of Teotihuacán is believed to have been brought about by the Chichimecs, a primitive, nomadic, Náhuatl-speaking people from the northern plains.

Following a period of chaos in central Mexico, the tenth century A.D. saw the rise of the Toltec city of Tula (also called Tollan). The worship of Quetzalcoatl reached peak proportions at Tula. The

Opposite, top: The massive Pyramid of the Sun at Teotihuacán
Bottom: At Teotihuacán, the Temple of Quetzalcoatl
or the plumed serpent, revered most highly by the Toltecs

legendary bearded white man had been immortalized by the Indian peoples as a creature half bird and half reptile, representing the elements of the sky and of the earth. In the Náhuatl language, the word *quetzal* means "bird" and *coatl* means "snake." The pyramid the Toltecs built to Quetzalcoatl at Tula was surmounted by a temple, the roof of which some archeologists believe was supported by immense figures of Toltec warriors. Although the roof is now gone, the warrior statues remain, stark and vivid against the sky. Low-relief carvings on the five-tiered pyramid are typically Toltec, showing stalking jaguars and coyotes and predatory birds consuming human hearts.

Despite the great powers that the Toltecs and others attributed to Quetzalcoatl, their god had an enemy. He was known as Tezcatlipoca, or "smoking mirror," and was presumably worshipped by the hostile Chichimecs. This evil god was so named because he was said to have a right foot of obsidian, a dark or smoky volcanic glass, and also because he represented that dark region to which the sun was believed to descend when it left the sky each evening.

In any case, as Tula grew into a wealthy city-state, Quetzalcoatl was neglected and the forces of Tezcatlipoca gained power. Sometime before the destruction of Tula by the Chichimecs, in the twelfth century A.D., the god-man who was the inspiration for the plumed serpent is said to have returned to the eastern coast of Mexico where he sailed out to sea on a raft made of serpents. He promised, however, to return and to do so in the year known as One Reed in the fifty-two-year cycle of the Indian calendar.

Another Indian legend foretold that a small band of nomadic people from the north would travel southward in search of a place of settlement in central Mexico where they would build a great city. They would know that they had reached the proper site when they came upon an eagle with a snake in its beak perched upon a nopal cactus growing from a rock located on an island in the middle of a lake.

The people were the Aztecs. Probably descended from a branch of the Chichimecs, they were also known as the México and as the Tenochcas, for the city they built on the islands of Lake Texcoco in the Valley of Mexico was Tenochtitlán. Its very name, in the Náhuatl language, means "cactus sprouting from a rock." So, in addition to giving the country of Mexico the name by which it is known today, the Aztec, or México, people gave it the eagle-and-cactus motif for the coat of arms that appears on its national flag.

The date of the founding of Tenochtitlán is usually given as A.D. 1325. Aztec culture borrowed much of its religion from the Toltecs, its art from the Mixtecs, and its knowledge of the calendar from the Maya. The Aztecs were, however, the most militaristic of the Indian civilizations, and their society was the most highly specialized. In addition to the ruling family and the divisions of the priesthood and of local governors, there were fixed categories of warriors, merchants, craftsmen, peasants, serfs, and others.

Among the numerous gods they worshipped were Tlaloc, Tezcatlipoca, and Quetzalcoatl. But the highest Aztec god was Huitzilopochtli, the god of the sun and of war. He demanded the greatest number of human sacrifices to insure that the sun would rise each morning, and as the Aztecs regarded themselves as the "people of the sun" they went to extreme lengths to satisfy his appetite for human blood. The other gods, too, had to be regularly appeased.

The ritual of human sacrifice usually began with the victim, escorted by priests, marching up the steps of the *teocalli*, or pyramid, playing a pottery flute. Once arrived at the god's temple on top, the victim was made to lie back across a large, drum-shaped stone, his body arched and his hands and feet held firmly to the ground by a group of priests. Another priest plunged an obsidian knife into his chest and tore out his heart, which was then offered to the temple god. The higher the rank of the victim the more effective his influence with the gods. Brave warriors were the most highly esteemed, and the Aztecs actually arranged ceremonial battles between groups

Drawing showing the ritual of human sacrifice
as practiced by the Aztecs (National Museum of Anthropology)

of captive Chichimecs and other peoples under their control in order to obtain worthy subjects for the temple altar. Death on the battlefield or on the sacrificial stone was regarded as the highest possible honor.

It seems doubtful that such a society, despite its fruitful fields, material riches, and genius for organization, could have flourished for very long. When the Spaniards arrived in 1519, Tenochtitlán had been enjoying its power and its supremacy over other Indian city-states for only a little more than a hundred years. Several factors account for Cortés' relatively easy conquest of the Aztec stronghold of perhaps as many as 300,000 people with an original landing force of only 500 or 600 men and 16 horses.

One element strongly in Cortés' favor was his arrival in a One Reed year, as foretold, which led the coastal peoples to send word of the return of Quetzalcoatl. The Spanish conquistador was white-skinned and bearded, and as the day of his landing was April 22, Good Friday on the Christian calendar in that year, he was dressed in solemn black and must have cut an imposing figure. The presence of horses was another psychological weapon. Although wild horses are believed to have crossed the Ice Age land bridge to the western hemisphere, they had become extinct long, long before and the Indians had never seen them. They thought, at first, that the horse and rider were one, a single supernatural figure of great power. To this day, the distinction between the caballero, or horseman, and the individual of lower status, the peon who must go on foot, prevails in Mexico. Cannons, gunpowder, armor, and other articles of worked metal were also, of course, awe-inspiring to the Indians.

Of direct help to the conquerors was the resentment of those peripheral peoples from whom the Aztecs had long been exacting tribute in both goods and human lives. They were quite ready to join with the Spanish in the destruction of their oppressors. Cortés also had the help of Malinche, a young Indian woman from the region of Tabasco who spoke the Aztec and Mayan tongues and soon learned Spanish so that she was able to act as translator from the time of the landing at Veracruz.

During the two years between April of 1519 and the final conquest of Tenochtitlán in August of 1521, Cortés and the Aztec rulers struggled for control. The king Moctecuhzoma II (better known as Moctezuma or Montezuma) had come to the throne in 1502. He was torn between two courses: that of following the dictates of the god Huitzilopochtli and making all-out war on the invaders or that of embracing the belief in the return of Quetzalcoatl and welcoming Cortés and his men. After rich gifts sent by messengers to the coast did not satisfy the Spanish leader or prevent his march to the highlands, Moctezuma permitted him and his party to enter the capital peacefully in November of 1519. Already, however, the Spanish forces had massacred thousands en route, at the Aztec city of Cholula where they had suspected a trap. And soon after entering Tenochtitlán, Cortés had Moctezuma himself imprisoned.

June of 1520 saw an uprising against the Spanish occupation of Tenochtitlán in which Moctezuma was stoned to death, presumably by his own people, while trying to quell the rioting. Cortés and his men then tried to steal out of the city but were set upon by the Indians in a bloody encounter known as La Noche Triste, "the sorrowful night" of June 30, 1520. Nearly three-fourths of the Spanish soldiers were killed and the rest made a rapid retreat. But in May of the following year, Cortés returned with reinforcements of new armaments, fresh Spanish recruits, and strong Indian allies. After a harsh siege of three months, Tenochtitlán fell. The city was virtually destroyed and subsequently Cuauhtémoc, the nephew of Moctezuma who had become the Aztec ruler, was put to death on the charge of conspiring against Cortés.

The great era of Mexico's Indian civilizations had come to a close. Although the influences of that period would reach far into the future, the next three hundred years were to witness the implantation of Spanish institutions—political, religious, economic, social—in the newly conquered land. Even its name, New Spain, reflected this European attempt at a complete takeover of its society. Yet, in the long run, neither the Indian nor the Spanish culture would predominate. Instead the two would blend, like hardy and stubborn substances in the intense heat of a crucible, to produce an entirely new culture, one that could only be described as Mexican and that would be unparalleled in the Americas.

From 1535, the ruler of the new colony was a viceroy directly responsible to the king of Spain. The boundaries of New Spain were still uncertain. Only partially explored and secured, they reached northward beyond the Rio Grande and southward into Central

A statue of Cortés, a rare sight in Mexico;
located on private grounds in Cuernavaca

America. The Spanish viceroy was assisted by a hierarchy of governors, mayors, and a large bureaucracy, all Spanish-born except in the very lowest ranks of office. But the main instrument of assistance to the viceregal administration, besides the ever-present military forces, was the church.

Priests of the Catholic faith accompanied Cortés on his expedition to Mexico. Spain itself had only recently, in 1492, succeeded in driving out the last of the Moorish invaders and was consolidating its diverse peoples under the Catholic monarchs, Ferdinand and Isabella. Church and state were one in the mother country, and the Spanish throne used the dread Inquisition—the examination of faith for heresy—to consolidate political power as well as for religious purposes. Enforcing conformity with church doctrine, although chiefly by methods other than the Inquisition, was to carry over into New Spain.

The practices of the Inquisition in Spain had included the burning of nonbelievers at the stake. But still the Catholic conquerors of Mexico found the Indian practice of human sacrifice to the gods

At the Shrine of the Virgin of Guadalupe: statuary depicting
the miracle of the holy image on Juan Diego's cloak

horrifying. In Tenochtitlán, they observed rows of heads of victims
impaled on pikes and reported the pyramid temples to be covered
with blood and stench. They even circulated rumors that Aztec
priests drank the blood and consumed parts of the bodies of the
slaughtered victims. Among the first acts of the Spanish soldiers and
clergy after the conquest was the partial dismantling of the pyramids, particularly their temples, and the building of churches, often
with the very same stones. In Cholula, the scene of the first major
massacre of Indians by the Spaniards, there are said to be 365
churches, one for each day of the year and nearly all built on the
sites of razed pyramid temples or other Aztec religious monuments.

Priests and missionaries of the various religious orders—Franciscan, Dominican, Augustinian, and later Jesuit—entered New Spain
in growing numbers. The transition from the Indian beliefs to
Catholicism was facilitated by the religious experience, in 1531, of a
recently converted fifty-five-year-old Indian who, having taken a
Spanish name, was known as Juan Diego. Diego reported that he
had seen the Virgin Mary at a place known as Guadalupe, on the
outskirts of Mexico City. The Virgin commanded him to take a

message to the city's recently appointed bishop requesting that a church be built at Guadalupe.

The bishop at first doubted Diego's story, and so the humble Indian returned to the spot where he had seen the Virgin. Once more she appeared to Diego, and now, where only cactus had grown earlier, roses came into bloom. Told by the Virgin to pick some of the blooms, Diego returned to the bishop with his cloak full of flowers. Yet when he opened his cloak before the bishop, the roses had vanished and in their place an image of the Virgin herself appeared on the cloth.

The church was, of course, built and the miraculous cloth of Diego's cape was hung over the altar. Our Lady of Guadalupe became the patron saint of Mexico, and December 12, the day of Diego's second vision, became Guadalupe Day throughout the country.

The acceptance of the new faith was in many ways quite natural for the Indians of New Spain. The churches with their domed interiors, gilded and painted altars, and images were an effective replacement for the imposing pyramids with their stone carvings and statues of the gods. Shrines like that of Guadalupe are to this day approached by the penitent inching forward for long distances on their knees, a practice perhaps not unrelated, for the Indians, to the ascent of holy parties up the steps of the pyramid. And churchyard fiestas, with their fireworks and pulque drinking, appear to be an extension of the spirited religious festivals once held in the forecourts of the larger pyramids.

Two Spanish priests of early colonial days who were protective of the Indians and their culture were Bartolomé de las Casas and Bernardino de Sahagún. The former tried to protect the human rights of this subject people, while the latter made an intensive study of the Náhuatl language and of Aztec traditions and customs to preserve them for posterity. In many cases, particularly among the Maya, Indian writings in codex form were wantonly destroyed

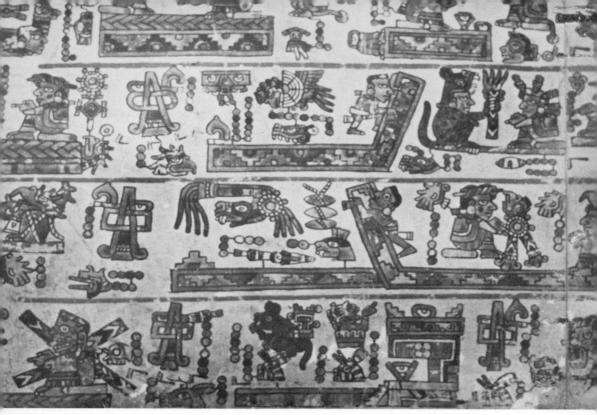

Portion of a Mixtec codex showing colored glyphs

by the military or by members of the clergy because they were believed to be a threat to the Christian religion. Not only the contents but the artistry of these codices, with their beautifully colored glyphs, were lost.

Las Casas fought unsuccessfully against the *encomienda,* a means of economic exploitation of the Indian whereby the owner of a hacienda or other enterprise became the lord and protector of his Indian laborers. The serflike workers who were "commended" to his care were paid little or nothing. In return for their services, the Spanish *patrón,* whether a member of the clergy or the laity, saw to their spiritual and bodily needs. This feudalistic system provided, in a sense, a substitute for the community after the breakdown of Indian society, but it was open to many abuses.

Another institution that had much potential for exploitation of the Indians was the *repartimiento,* through which the Spanish were given the right to round up Indian labor to be apportioned to perform specific jobs. Although the Indians were to be paid for this work, again abuses were common and the *repartimiento* often amounted to a system of forced labor.

Economically, Mexico expanded during the colonial period. Mining, cattle raising, and new agricultural crops of commercial value such as sugarcane and wheat were introduced. Although the conquistadores had come to the New World mainly for gold and silver (and indeed Mexico did yield such mineral riches), the real wealth of New Spain proved to be its land and its Indian labor. In the colonies of the Caribbean, South America, and the future United States, most of the Indians had not been farmers primarily, and they tended to die or run off when pressed into field labor. As a result, black slaves were imported from Africa.

Although the Indian population of Mexico did suffer considerable losses through the conquest, the indigenous labor force remained large, and relatively few African slaves were brought to New Spain. Of course, not all of Mexico's Indian population was pressed into working for the Spanish conquerors. In the far north, in the remote mountains, and in the southern jungles numerous pockets of Indian peoples continued to pursue their nomadic, hunting way of life or to till their own small fields. But, in general, on the haciendas and in the mines, under difficult working conditions and for long hours, the many toiled for the profits of the few.

By the early 1800's, three hundred years after the conquest, the population of New Spain was sharply stratified into classes—really castes—based on circumstances of birth. At the top of the political, religious, social, and economic ladder were the *peninsulares,* people of pure Spanish blood born on the Iberian Peninsula. Less flatteringly, they were known as *gachupines,* a word taken from the Náhuatl and meaning "wearers of spurs." On the rung just beneath this most privileged class were the *criollos,* or creoles, born of

Spanish parents but in New Spain rather than in the mother country. Next came the mestizos, of mixed Spanish and Indian blood. And, lastly, still greatest in number, came the Indians. In the early 1800's they made up 60 percent of the population.

Discontent with Spanish rule had been growing, mainly among the *criollos*, who numbered about half a million and who particularly resented the top advantages enjoyed by the *peninsulares*. Also, the Spanish crown had long been exploiting the colony economically. The throne exacted one-fifth, known as the king's fifth, of the wealth of New Spain in metals and gems. In addition, Spain forbade the cultivation of grapes or olives, the mining of salt, or the establishment of silk culture in New Spain. The mother country held a monopoly on these enterprises and forced the colony to buy its wine, olive oil, salt, and silk exclusively from Spain.

In 1808, the Spanish king temporarily lost his throne through Napoleon's invasion and occupation of Spain, and in New Spain the *criollos*, supported by the mestizos and the Indians, rose in favor of independence. They were stirred by the recent, successful Revolutionary War in the United States and also by the French Revolution. On September 16, 1810, the first blow was struck by a *criollo* priest, Father Miguel Hidalgo of the town of Dolores, about 150 miles north of Mexico City. His call to arms, the famous Grito de Dolores, or Cry from Dolores, proclaimed loyalty to the Virgin of Guadalupe and vowed freedom from the tyranny of the *gachupines*.

With an ill-equipped army of about 50,000, Hidalgo started to march toward the capital but was stopped by forces loyal to the crown. He withdrew to Guadalajara but was captured some months later, tried by the Inquisition, stripped of his priestly office, and, in July of 1811, he was shot. His severed head, along with those of other insurgents, was placed on public view as a warning to any who might think of challenging the king's authority.

Another eleven years passed before the goal of independence was achieved. Among those insurgent heroes who died in the struggle for freedom from Spanish rule, racial equality, and the abolition of class privilege was another priest, Father José María Morelos. Morelos advocated specific social reforms as well, including the distribution of privately held lands to the peasants. Like Hidalgo, Morelos was condemned by the Inquisition and shot to death in 1815.

When independence from Spain did come, in 1821, it arrived, oddly enough, in the form of a Mexican monarchy. The short-term emperor, known as Agustín I, had been a *criollo* army officer named Agustín de Iturbide, who had first fought against the insurgents and then switched his allegiance and joined with the insurgent general, Vincente Guerrero. Agustín lost his "empire" in 1823 when the Central American states broke away, his troubled government collapsed, and he was forced to abdicate. The following year, 1824, Mexico was proclaimed a republic and given a constitution patterned after that of the United States.

Mural by Diego Rivera depicting revolutionary struggle; figures in pointed hats are being tried by Inquisition (National Palace, Mexico City)

A president was elected, a former insurgent named Félix Fernández, who took the name of Guadalupe Victoria in honor of the long struggle for independence. The national flag was designed, a green, white, and red vertical tricolor. Superimposed on the white ground was the Aztec motif: an eagle with a snake in its beak perched on a rock from which a cactus plant sprang. But political stability was still a long way off. The series of inept presidents that followed Guadalupe Victoria was succeeded by a militaristic and opportunistic dictator-president, General Antonio López de Santa Anna.

Between 1833 and 1855, although he was frequently deposed and even exiled, Santa Anna managed to hold the office of president of Mexico numerous times. During his despotic and corrupt regime, Mexico lost Texas, which declared itself independent in 1836, and fought the Mexican War of 1846-48. The latter resulted in the loss of all Mexico's territory north and west of the Rio Grande. Santa Anna's attack on Texans at the Alamo in 1836 and the invasion of Mexico by a United States expeditionary force during the Mexican War bred hostility between the two countries. By the time Santa Anna's power was broken, Mexico was in a state of near chaos. Nor had most of the goals of the independence movement of 1810 been realized. The *criollos* like Santa Anna and the earlier presidents of the republic had become the new privileged class, along with the traditionally wealthy and influential clergy, and the mestizos and the Indians continued to suffer discrimination and poverty.

La Reforma, the reform movement, was initiated in Mexico, very fittingly, by a leader of its Indian population, Benito Juárez. A full-blooded Zapotec from the state of Oaxaca, Juárez rose from domestic service as a houseboy to the study of law, to various Government posts, and finally to the presidency. His struggle in the liberal cause, supported by the nation's mestizo and Indian majority, began in the late 1850's with his Leyes de Reforma, or Laws of Reform.

Their goal was to restrict privilege and redistribute the wealth,

A large, free-standing mosaic panel at Oaxaca,
illustrating the life of Benito Juárez, leader of the reform movement

particularly the extensive landholdings of the church, which made
up nearly half of Mexico's cultivable acreage. As set forth in the
constitution of 1857, the reform laws separated church and state,
guaranteed religious liberty, instituted mandatory civil registration
of all births, marriages, and deaths, established public, state-directed
education, suppressed religious orders, and forbade religious taxa-
tion.

The Juárez who was elected president of Mexico in 1861 was a
Lincolnlike figure, a somber statesman of humble origin who
dressed in a simple black suit and cloak, wore the stovepipe hat that
was fashionable at the time, and was deeply admired by the common people. His administration had the support of the United States,
but that country had just become engaged in its Civil War. Meantime, in Mexico, the church and the landowners were taking steps
to unseat Juárez.

They appealed to Emperor Napoleon III of France for a foreign monarch who would take control of Mexico and restore their power and prosperity. The forces of Juárez struggled against the invading French army and won a victory at Puebla on May 5, 1862. But the French were only temporarily beaten, and, in 1864, they succeeded in driving Juárez from the capital and installing the Austrian archduke, Maximilian, as emperor of Mexico. The reign of Maximilian and his wife, Carlota, was brief and ill-fated. Soon after the close of the Civil War in the United States, the French army was withdrawn and, in 1867, Maximilian was executed. Juárez returned to the presidency until his death in 1872.

The intrusion of the foreign monarchs had, if anything, strengthened Mexican unity and elevated Juárez to the position of a beloved

The Fort of Loreto near Puebla where the French army was dealt a temporary setback on May 5, 1862

national figure. But most of his reforms were ahead of their time and did not become fully implemented for many decades. In fact, the next prominent Mexican leader, Porfirio Díaz, swung to a more conservative position favoring the church and the landowners.

Like Juárez, Díaz came from Oaxaca and in his early days had been active in La Reforma and in the overthrow of Emperor Maximilian. He was a mestizo, part Mixtec Indian. But during the thirty-five years of his regime, from 1876 to 1911, he became the patron of the land barons, the industrialists, and the wealthy foreign investors, mainly from the United States. He was also a strict disciplinarian with little sympathy for the plight of the peasants and laborers.

True, the *porfiriato*, as his period of government was known, saw the development of railroads, telephone and telegraph systems, electrification, and public utilities. Oil was discovered on the Gulf Coast, and the port of Tampico and the city of Monterrey boomed. But, as the church lands and privileges were restored and the great haciendas of the north grew even wealthier, the landless peasantry (about 90 percent of the rural population) was pressed into peonage. Virtually prisoners of the landowners, the peons lived and worked on the estate, bought their necessities in the estate store, and were kept perpetually in debt because of their inadequate wages.

The peon who tried to protest or run away would be brought to swift punishment by Díaz' rural police force, known as the rurales. While these well-armed, mounted patrol forces did much to stamp out banditry and lawlessness in the countryside and to make travel safe, the rurales were also a convenient tool for the suppression of disobedient citizens and political enemies. *Porfirianismo* not only bled the masses; it ruthlessly stripped the country of resources like oil, timber, gold, silver, and copper. Yet Díaz managed to give Mexico the appearance of overall prosperity as he beautified the towns with bandstands, built the impressive Palacio da las Bellas

Diego Rivera's depiction of Porfirio Díaz with a female figure
personifying the Mexico that he both adorned and bled
(Hotel del Prado, Mexico City)

Artes theater and museum in Mexico City, expanded industrial
activity, and kept the railroads running on time.

Clearly a new revolutionary era was due. It began on November
20, 1910, when a wealthy landowner, Francisco I. Madero, rose to
protest Díaz' dictatorial behavior (he had had himself reelected

seven times) and his yielding of so much of Mexico's wealth to foreign interests. Díaz, now over eighty years old, departed the country for Europe in 1911, leaving the field wide open for an assortment of idealists, militarists, bandit-generals, and genuine reformers who attempted to take control of the chaotic scene. Mexico's rugged landscape provided natural barriers for the strongholds of such colorful figures as Francisco (Pancho) Villa in the north and Emiliano Zapata in the south, whose private armies of "liberation" roved the countryside attacking and looting churches and haciendas.

In 1913, after a brief presidency, Madero was shot and the counterrevolutionary General Victoriano Huerta came to office. The United States was suspected of political intervention on his behalf for the purpose of preserving its big-business investments in Mexico. Huerta was replaced by Venustiano Carranza, who framed the con-

A portrayal of the spirit of the Revolution of 1910
in a mural painting by the militant artist, David Alfaro Siqueiros

stitution of 1917, the leading document of the Revolution of 1910, and who served as president until his death by assassination in 1920. The constitution incorporated many of the principles of La Reforma plus new social legislation to benefit the peasants and the growing number of industrial workers.

The next president, Alvaro Obregón, tried to consolidate the three power groups of the Revolution: the independent generals, the land reformers, and the new labor leaders. He began the systematic redistribution of land, mainly in the form of *ejidos*—farming acreage for communal use to be administered by village cooperatives. Obregón also fostered pride in the increasingly dominant mestizo quality of Mexican society through public education and through public support of the great mural painters—Rivera, Orozco, Siqueiros —who produced vivid and detailed picture stories that told of the history, traditions, and culture of the Mexican people.

The Revolution of 1910 was bloody and prolonged. By 1923, four of its five major figures—Madero, Zapata, Carranza, and Villa—had met violent deaths. In 1928, the fifth—Obregón—was murdered. But an era of peace and stability was ushered in in 1934 by President Lázaro Cárdenas, a Tarascan Indian. A new law was passed that extended the four-year term of the Mexican president to six and prohibited reelection. Serving for all six years, Cárdenas greatly expanded the distribution of *ejido* lands and brought the railroads under the control of a Government-supervised agency. Most notable, he nationalized Mexico's oil fields and refineries, thus breaking free of a major source of foreign economic domination. Also, as the danger of church control of secular matters was now past, Cárdenas relaxed the rule prohibiting religious education for those who desired it.

The presidents that followed Cárdenas in single, orderly six-year terms of office have for the most part tried to realize the goals of the 1910 Revolution, with social-welfare programs, public-works improvements, land distribution, agricultural and industrial development, and the preservation of Mexico's political and economic independence, particularly with regard to its powerful neighbor to the north. Some leaders have steered a middle-of-the-road course politically; others have veered slightly to the left or to the right. In general, they have balanced each other; a president who has favored the nation's private business interests has usually been followed by one more oriented to the needs of the country's poor.

Class divisions based on racial factors sparked the independence movement of 1810 and the reform movement of the 1850's, and they were responsible for many of the economic issues that ignited the Revolution of 1910. Today these divisions have blurred considerably. Since 1920, *mestizaje*, the mixing of Mexico's Spanish and Indian elements both ethnically and culturally, has gained momentum. The crucible process, however, is not complete. Mexico is currently a land of three cultures: that of the distant past, that of the more recent past, and that of the present. It is intriguing to seek out and rewarding to explore those Indian, Spanish, and contemporary features that make the Mexican cultural scene so unique.

3 Land of Three Cultures

Visitors to Mexico City are often taken to the Plaza of the Three Cultures to view a site that was formerly an Aztec marketplace and ceremonial center. The bases of the ruined pyramids are neighbors to a Spanish church built in 1536. It was constructed partly of porous, reddish-brown *tezontle*, a lightweight stone of volcanic origin widely used by the Indians. Surrounding the plaza is a group of residential and office buildings in sleek, contemporary style, typical of modern Mexico City.

The three-culture vista is repeated over and over again in the bustling streets of the capital and other major cities where Indian vendors of fruits, snacks, and flowers sit among their wares spread forth on the sidewalks. Often in the background are churches and older public buildings with tiled domes and facades, iron grillwork decoration, vaulting bell towers, and quiet interior patios that are strongly reminiscent of Spain. Such scenes are accented by neon-lighted billboards, unceasing motor traffic, and many other evidences of twentieth-century technology.

The root culture of Mexico—that of the Indian—is still strongly alive, however, even though people of pure Indian stock, known as *naturales*, are diminishing in number all the time and now probably make up between 5 and 7 percent of the population (which presently totals about sixty-three million). The Indian presence is also seen, of course, in the mestizo faces of well over 80, perhaps even 90, percent of Mexicans.

Most of the nation's Indian peoples are found in pockets of the country that are remote from its center, in areas that were relatively undisturbed by the Spanish conquest and that remained virtually sealed off from the mainstream of Mexican life for centuries. These sections include the Chiapas highlands, the Isthmus of Tehuantepec, the mountain heights encircling Oaxaca, parts of the Sierra Madres and the Meseta Central, and the Yucatán Peninsula. There are still about eighty different Indian languages and dialects spoken in Mexico (although there were once nearly two hundred). The Náhuatl of the Aztecs plus the Mayan, Zapotec, and Mixtec tongues are still predominant among Indian speakers, just as they were in Cortés' day. And there are dozens of tongues used by smaller population groups. Some groups are tiny, numbering only a few hundred people, and their languages are almost certainly doomed to extinction.

An Indian child from the mountain heights encircling Oaxaca; she is holding a box of picnic scraps given her by a passing motorist and intended for her puppy

In addition to Mexico's shrinking Indian population, there is a substantial segment of the mestizo population that, according to the Government, "follows an Indian way of life." Members of this group usually speak Spanish, the official language of Mexico, rather than an Indian language, or they may be bilingual. But other cultural boundaries tend to be fuzzy. They share the poverty of the Indians, barely subsisting in tiny rural communities, despite their ability to speak Spanish and their acceptance of certain European institutions such as the church. Many *naturales* as well as mestizos practice what is known as "folk Catholicism," Roman Catholic rituals tinged with a heavy measure of Indian beliefs and superstitions.

In the Indian regions, weekly open-air markets called *tianguis* are held, often on Sunday and sometimes in conjunction with church-going. In Oaxaca, the center for many Zapotec and Mixtec peoples from the surrounding area, an Indian market is held daily. But Saturday is the principal shopping day. In a scene that is as colorful

At the Saturday market in Oaxaca where most patrons are Indians

Huichol Indians visiting
the National Museum of Anthropology in Mexico City

as it is congested, the crowds converge on the street stalls that form
a large cross at one of the intersections near the center of the city.
Fruits, vegetables, spices, chickens, medicinal herbs, blankets, plas-
tic toys, clothing, and household articles are among the items offered
for sale. The *tiangui* is not only a place for socializing and trading,
it often provides the point of contact between the Indian culture
and the influences of modern Mexico.

Very few Indian groups have remained as culturally isolated as
the Huichol, a Náhuatl-speaking people who live in the high pine
forests of the Sierra Madre Occidental, in the states of Nayarit and
Jalisco. Once a nomadic hunting people, the Huichol turned to the
cultivation of corn to keep from starvation after the wildlife of their
area began to be killed off by the encroachment of ranching and

mining operations. The Huichol still use digging sticks and other primitive tools to plant their corn, beans, and squash in steep mountain clearings. To ensure good harvests, they court the gods of nature with animal sacrifices and elaborate ceremonies. They have often been called the "people of the peyote" because of their use of the hallucinogenic drug derived from the peyote cactus. And they are also noted for the elaborate designs with which they paint their faces. The Huichol way of life is probably one of the best-preserved Indian cultures of Mexico.

Since the Revolution of 1910, Mexico's Indian heritage has been the key factor in the promotion of Mexican nationalism. It has provided the inspiration for the country's great mural painters, for the vibrant dance compositions of its world-famous Ballet Folklórico, for the mosaic facades of the National University buildings in Mexico City, and for the capital's exceptionally splendid National Museum of Anthropology.

The most hallowed of historical figures is Cuauhtémoc, the last Aztec emperor and the Indian whose death meant "not a victory nor a defeat, but the painful birth of the mestizo nation that is today Mexico." So reads the plaque marking the site of the Indian ruler's fall from power at the hands of the Spanish conquerors. Statues of Cuauhtémoc are a common sight in the country's cities and towns, while representations of Hernán Cortés are exceedingly rare. Yet one of the contradictions of Mexican life is that, despite the high tribute paid to the cultural heritage of the Indian, in actuality he occupies the very lowest position on the economic and social scale in today's Mexico.

The Spanish conquest imposed many new cultural factors upon the civilization of the Indians. Language, law, religion, education, transportation, architecture, handicrafts, foods, dress, manners, work and recreational patterns all quickly began to reflect the influence of the Europeans. In proportion to the number of Spaniards that emigrated to New Spain, the impact was enormous. It is estimated

Mexico City's *zócalo* with 17th-century cathedral (at left)
and adjoining sanctuary buildings with ornate facade

that during the 300-year colonial period, the influx from the mother
country added up to only about 300,000 people.

If this figure is correct, then presumably the mestizo of modern
Mexico is predominantly of Indian ancestry. The first mestizos were
the offspring, in almost every case, of Spanish fathers and Indian
mothers. And succeeding generations probably resulted mainly from
unions between mestizos or between mestizos and Indians. Yet
Mexico's mestizo culture shows the Spanish influence in its background more strongly than its Indian roots.

The first colonial towns of New Spain, with their narrow cobbled
streets and central plazas, resembled the towns of the mother
country and have retained that look to this day. The Spanish word
zócalo, meaning "base or pedestal" (as of a column), has taken over
in Mexico to mean "plaza." The colonial houses and other buildings,

too, were Spanish in flavor, with tiled floors and roofs and central courtyards, while the churches of New Spain followed the succeeding styles of Spanish religious architecture, running the gamut from the heavy and almost grim Romanesque and Gothic to the exuberant and richly decorative baroque.

The Indian acceptance of the Roman Catholic religion, with its many rituals and saints, has been explained largely by its parallelism to the Indian religions with their many gods. It also seems plausible that the Virgin Mary occupies a similar role to the Aztec mother of the gods, known as Tonantzin. Interestingly, the place where the Indian, Juan Diego, first reported seeing the Virgin was on a site sacred to Tonantzin. And often the Virgin of Guadalupe is depicted as dark-skinned and with Indian features.

Although church and state are officially separate in Mexico, in

Spanish architecture in Puebla showing characteristic tiling, stuccowork, and iron grillwork

The sharply tilted 17th-century Basilica of Guadalupe,
closed to the public in 1976

the wake of the reforms inaugurated by Juárez over a century ago,
between 80 and 90 percent of the population follows the Catholic
faith (and 2 to 3 percent are Protestants). The original church of
the Virgin of Guadalupe was replaced by a larger building that was
begun around 1685 and completed in 1709. Known as the Basilica

of Guadalupe, its fame grew and by the present century it was attracting some six million Mexicans annually. However, the building had for some time been sinking into the soft, lake-bed subsoil underlying Mexico City. It had become sharply tilted and developed large cracks, making it unsafe for occupancy.

In October of 1976, a new Basilica of Guadalupe adjacent to the old one, was dedicated. Built in large part with the pesos of the poor and devout, the new structure faces on the same massive square, often bloodstained with the bruised knees of approaching penitents. It is less ornate than the former basilica but can hold 10,000 worshippers and, of course, now houses the sacred image of the Virgin. As the dedication of the new basilica was concerned strictly with the country's religious life, the Mexican Government did not participate officially in the ceremony. Yet there is no denying that the devotion to the church formed under the Spanish influence of the colonial era continues to be a major aspect of Mexican life.

In Mexico's civil and criminal codes of law, in its currency (the peso, or weight, named after the peseta of Spain), in its everyday customs, such as the siesta, or afternoon nap (sometimes abbreviated to a long lunch hour), in its manners and courtesies including its effusive *abrazos* (embraces accompanied by kisses on the cheek that are exchanged by men as well as women), the country further exhibits its adoption of Spanish ways.

Most Mexicans bear Spanish rather than Indian names, and the format of their names follows the Spanish pattern. The Mexican president, José López-Portillo y Pacheco, for example, uses both his father's surname (López Portillo) and his mother's maiden surname (Pacheco). A married woman can have a long string of names, often using the surnames of one or both of her parents *and* one of her husband's parents, with a *de* before the latter. The Mexican president's wife, having omitted one of her parents' surnames, calls herself Carmen Romano de López Portillo.

The Spanish occupation literally put the colony on horseback, or at least on burro back, and also gave it the horse, mule, and donkey to serve as beasts of burden. Formerly, all goods had been carried on human backs. The new enterprise of cattle ranching gave rise to the cowboy culture. The first mounted vaqueros were Indians or mestizos. They developed the skills of roping, branding, and rounding up cattle and later passed them on to the European-descended cowboys of the United States. Words like *rodeo*, *corral*, *lasso* (from the Spanish *lazo*), and *lariat* (*la reata*) all found their way into usage in the United States through the Mexican cowherds who worked on the haciendas north of the Rio Grande in the years before Texan independence and the Mexican War.

Bullfighting, the Spanish (and Portuguese) spectacle believed to have originated in ancient Crete, is more strongly entrenched in

An amateur bullfight in an improvised country bullring

A professional bullfight in Mexico City

Mexico than anywhere else in Latin America. In New Spain, the first bullfight (more correctly called a *corrida de toros*, or "running of the bulls") was held in 1529. Mexico City today has the largest bullring in the world, the Plaza Monumental, which seats 50,000 people, and about 200 other rings are found around the country. The fighting bulls are descended from Spanish breeding stock, and the matadors, banderilleros, and picadors, in their rich and colorful costumes, follow all the rules of the contest as presented in Spain. Mexican bullfights take place on Sundays throughout the season, which runs from November through March. At other times, novilladas, contests with young bulls and less experienced bullfighters, can usually be seen.

The introduction of cattle, horses, pigs, and sheep provided New Spain with leather and wool. The garments of the Indians had been chiefly of cotton, sometimes of pounded tree bark or woven cactus fiber. Cloaks, needed for warmth, were of deerskin or other wild-animal hides, even of layers of straw. After the Spanish conquest, the horsemen of Mexico dressed in leather extensively. They used it also, of course, for their saddles and other riding gear.

The classic horseman's, or *charro*, costume of colonial Mexico was of doeskin or other supple leather and consisted of high-waisted riding trousers and a short bolero jacket trimmed with rows of silver buttons or decorated with braid. A frilled shirt, spurred boots, and a wide-brimmed sombrero completed the outfit. Later Mexico's strolling mariachi musicians adopted the Spanish-inspired *charro* costume. Nowadays it is usually of dark cloth decorated with silver studs. The leather *charro* costume may still be seen, however, on the gentleman and lady riders who appear in Mexico's rodeolike *charreadas*, performing roping skills and other fancy horsemanship on finely trained steeds. *Charreadas* are usually presented to the public on Sundays in Mexico City and at fiestas.

The "national" costume of Mexican women is called the *china poblana*, which translates as "Chinese girl of Puebla," because it is believed to have first been worn by a servant girl in that city who was of Chinese origin. Nonetheless, it is primarily Spanish in style, consisting of an embroidered white blouse and a full red-and-green skirt with embroidered or sequinned trim. Underneath the skirt there may be several fancy white petticoats. The red, white, and green colors are those of the Mexican flag. The *china poblana* is worn with a rebozo, a stole of silk, cotton, or wool thrown over the shoulders. This garment can also be used to cover the head in church or elsewhere and provides a handy sling for a baby or for gathering up market goods.

The colorful and decorative *china poblana* is seldom seen nowadays except at costume balls, fiestas, and other special events. In everyday life, Mexican women tend to wear either contemporary dress or, among rural people and the poorer classes, an adaptation of Spanish peasant dress, consisting of a short-sleeved blouse, long, semifull skirt, and the ever-useful rebozo. The counterpart for the man is the simple peon's outfit of homemade trousers of unbleached cotton, known as *calzones*, loose-fitting cotton shirt, sombrero, and huaraches, sandals made of interwoven leather thongs. The serape, a wool blanket carried over the shoulder, replaces the animal-hide cloak of the Indian and can be opened up to envelop the entire body in cold or wet weather. On the tropical Gulf Coast from Veracruz south and also in the Yucatán, men wear the cool *guayabera*, a shirt of lightweight, semisheer cotton that falls outside the trousers. In more elegant versions, the *guayabera* is embellished with fine pleating, several pockets, and elaborate embroidery work.

None of these garments is representative of Mexico's Indian heritage. In pre-Hispanic times men wore loincloths and capes and women dressed in long shifts (the *huipil*) that were basically rectangles with openings for the head and arms. Trousers were unknown, and the principal kinds of headgear were fashioned of feathers. Among the Maya of the Yucatán, however, it is still possible to see women dressed in long white tunic dresses, embroidered at the neck and hem, that are reminiscent of the Indian past.

The several kinds of hats that are considered typically Mexican are of Spanish origin, with adaptations developed for the various regional climates and customs. There are the utilitarian felt cowboy hats of the northern plains and the extravagantly designed *charro* hats of the state of Jalisco. The latter, with their high conical crowns and wide brims, usually supply the "centerpiece" for the Mexican hat dance. In hot, humid Veracruz, the hat of lightweight, loosely woven palm straw, with a deep, pinched crown and a curving brim, is favored for protection against the sun, while in the Yucatán the more finely woven Panama straw, made in fact from an Ecuadorian fiber, is preferred. Even the remote Huichol Indians have taken to wearing a kind of straight-brimmed hat, adding ribbons or other decorations that hang down fringelike from the brim. Possibly it is

Left: The decorated Indian *huipil* worn over a longer underdress
(Regional Museum of Oaxaca)
Right: Ruffled lace headdress from Tehuantepec (at left)
and peon's loose cotton shirt and *calzones* (Regional Museum of Oaxaca)

an adaptation of the low-crowned, beribboned men's hats of the neighboring state of Michoacán.

Also noteworthy for their headgear are the Indian women of the Isthmus of Tehuantepec, who at festival times appear in unusual pleated cotton or ruffled lace headdresses that serve as both head covering and cape. Probably not of Indian derivation at all, these lavish and extraordinary garments appear to have been inspired by the Spanish mantilla.

Mexico's food is truly "mestizo" in its blending of Indian and Spanish elements, each enhancing the other, expanding its uses and enlivening its flavors. Corn, the basis of Indian life, supplied the Indians with their bread, the tortilla. This thin, flexible pancake was prepared from hulled, dried corn kernels boiled in water and then rolled into a doughy mass or paste known as masa. The Indian

The metate and stone rolling pin used for grinding corn into masa
to make tortillas (Regional Museum of Oaxaca)

women knelt at a metate, a large stone slab sometimes raised on
three short stone legs, to perform the daily chore of mashing the
kernels smooth with a stone "rolling pin." They then pinched off
chunks of masa, deftly shaped and slapped them into large round
wafers, and toasted them on a clay griddle over an open fire.

The Aztecs are said to have made their tortillas exceptionally
large, perhaps a foot in diameter. The tortilla served the Indians as
an edible scoop for another one of their daily foods, beans, known
since colonial times by their Spanish name, frijoles. The bean
varieties of the New World were more numerous than those of
Europe. They came in several sizes and in red, pink, brown, black,
and cream colors; some were even pinto, or spotted.

A third ingredient of the staple Indian diet was the chili pepper.
Dozens of kinds were cultivated, ranging in pod size from that of
a peanut to that of a large pear, in color from vivid reds, yellows,

and oranges to brilliant greens, and in flavor from mild to fiery. A sprinkling of dried chili pepper gave the bland-tasting corn tortillas and the boiled dried beans some bite and snap. *Pozole* was an Indian porridge or stew of whole or ground corn and water, and *atole* a beverage made with masa and water. Masa could also be shaped into a thick patty and wrapped in cornhusks into a "bundle," or tamale, derived from the Spanish word *tamal*, which was then cooked by steaming. The cornhusk was not eaten, only the cereal paste inside it.

While the Indians had chocolate, their only sweetener was honey from wild bees, and it probably did not occur to them to try to sweeten this bitter and oily product of the cacao bean. So they used chocolate as a pungent flavoring ingredient for meats instead. The dish the Mexicans call *mole poblano* is turkey or chicken served with mole (mó-lay) sauce, cooked in the style of Puebla. Its origins may be traced to the pre-Hispanic era when domesticated turkey or wild fowl was eaten with a smooth, dark-colored sauce made of pounded chocolate, chili peppers, green and red tomatoes, pumpkin seeds, peanuts, herbs, and other native flavorings. *Pipián*, also a sauce for fowl, was made from ground chilies, peanuts, and squash seeds. Avocados, pumpkins, sweet potatoes, pineapples, guavas, other fruits and vegetables, including the edible fruits and leaves of the nopal cactus, and game rounded out the Indian diet.

The arrival of Cortés brought about the birth of a Mexican cuisine. Plant and animal foods that were formerly unknown in the western hemisphere contributed zest, variety, and nutritive value to the Indian dietary staples. Corn and bean dishes were made more flavorful through the addition of onions, garlic, and olives. They were also protein enriched with beef, pork, poultry, eggs, cheese, and milk, a result of the introduction of cattle, pigs, and chickens, as well as sheep and goats. Wheat and rice from Europe expanded the variety of grains beyond corn and gave Mexico its first European breads. Raised loaves were formerly unknown because cornmeal lacked the elasticity of wheat flour and could not hold air. Fruits like oranges, lemons, and grapes offered a juiciness and tang that complemented the dryness and spiciness of many Indian foods. And sugar changed chocolate and vanilla into appealing flavorings that were soon much in demand for sweets and confections.

Once Spanish-introduced ingredients were added to the Indian tortilla, the enchilada, the taco, and the tostada came into being. The enchilada is a tortilla splashed with a spicy sauce containing ground chili peppers and heaped with chopped cooked beef, shredded chicken, or sausage, and/or grated cheese, frijoles, olives, minced onion, and shredded lettuce. The tortilla is then rolled up around the filling. A folded-over tortilla, fried crisp and filled with a choice of these ingredients, is a taco, while a tortilla fried crisp and flat and topped with a savory mixture of the above is a tostada.

Indian vegetables and spices for sale at the Oaxaca outdoor market

Made with wheat flour instead of masa, and wrapped around a filling, a tortilla becomes a *burrito*. And classic Indian tamales filled with cereal paste are made tastier and more nutritious with dabs of seasoned chicken or pork filling added to their centers. Indian *pozole*, with Spanish ingredients added, becomes a hearty pork, corn, and vegetable soup.

Boiled dried beans, another Indian dish, became *frijoles fritos* (fried beans) and *frijoles refritos* (refried beans) under Spanish culinary influence. The former are cooked beans mashed with a small amount of liquid and fried to a thick mush. *Frijoles refritos* are seasoned with garlic, salt, and chili powder and fried in lard or other fat until crisp-edged. Rice, once it had been introduced by the Spanish, became a Mexican everyday food, eaten along with frijoles and tortillas, especially by the poor.

Two other dishes that are regarded as typically Mexican, because they once again blend indigenous and Spanish ingredients, are guacamole and *seviche*. The former is a mash of ripe avocados seasoned with the chili peppers and tomatoes of the Indians and the onions, garlic, and lemon juice of Spain. *Seviche* is raw fish from Mexican waters marinated in chilies, garlic, onion, herbs, and lime juice. The lime juice acts on the protein in the fish, firming and whitening the flesh in a kind of "cooking" process without heat, and the dish is served chilled.

Sweets and desserts, virtually unknown in pre-Hispanic Mexico, owe their existence to the introduction and cultivation of sugarcane. Fruit pastes of guava, quince, and apple, whole small fruits such as strawberries coated in crystallized sugar, and small, rich cakes containing grated coconut and ground nuts are popular confections. Flan, a caramelized milk-and-egg custard, is adapted directly from Spanish cookery.

For non-Mexicans, the appeal of the country's cuisine has been tempered somewhat by warnings against drinking the water and eating fruits and vegetables that are not protected by thick skins

Sweet cakes and rolls on display at an Indian market

that can be peeled off. Such precautions are essential because of the centuries-old Mexican practice of using human wastes as agricultural fertilizer. Such wastes can contaminate food and water and bring on severe gastrointestinal illness, especially for the uninitiated.

The practice of fertilizing with human wastes began early in the pre-Hispanic era, probably because the Indians lacked those domesticated farm animals that, in other societies, proved a good source of manure. By the time the Spanish conquerors arrived, most Indian peoples had a built-up resistance to dysentery and related disturbances. Both custom and rural poverty have been responsible for the continued use of human fertilizer on small farms in today's Mexico. As a result, colas and other soft drinks have become highly popular with the Mexicans, as well as with many visitors to the country. Mexico also produces high-quality commercial beers, and pulque is the longtime standby of the Mexican worker.

Mexico's strong religious heritage and tempestuous national history have given it an abundance of holidays. Most celebrations are marked by intense gaiety—music, decorations, dancing, feasting, and drinking, punctuated by the staccato bursts of fireworks. The Mexican affinity for elaborate noisemakers seems to go back as far as the days of the Spanish conquest, when the gunpowder of the Europeans so impressed the Indians. Possibly it also appeared to them that loud bursts of sound were a means of driving off evil spirits. At any rate, the *castillo*, a "castle" or tower strung with firecrackers tied to a reed or wooden framework, is a feature of many fiestas. The *castillo's* explosives are so arranged as to go off a few at a time, prolonging the effect.

The piñata is another feature of Mexican celebrations. It is a clay jug, sometimes in the form of an animal, that contains sweets, toys, and other small presents. The piñata, covered with layers of colored paper, is usually dangled above the heads of blindfolded guests at a party, at Christmas or other times, or over revelers in a village square. Each tries to break the piñata with a long stick and bring its contents tumbling down.

January 1, New Year's Day, is flanked by two Christmas celebrations, that of December 25, marking the birth of Christ, and that of January 6, known as Twelfth Night or Epiphany, which celebrates the visit of the Three Wise Men (Los Santos Reyes, or The Holy Kings) to the infant Jesus. As early as December 16 the Christmas plays and religious ceremonies relating to the *nacimiento*, the birth of Jesus, have begun. For the next nine nights, the *posada* may be enacted. The word means "inn" or "lodging place," and the ceremony commemorates the wanderings of Mary and Joseph just prior to the birth of the Christ child. In a candle-lighted procession, people impersonating the homeless strangers knock at the doors of village houses and chant several stanzas of a religious dialogue with those within. In the larger cities, guests at Christmas parties may perform the *posada*.

The crèche rather than the Christmas tree is the symbol for the December 25 holiday in Mexico. However, modern influences, particularly from the United States, account for the growing popularity of the Christmas tree and for the exchange of Christmas cards and gifts on the *nacimiento*. Formerly Los Santos Reyes, January 6, was the day for the exchange of gifts. It was customary to leave empty shoes on doorsteps and window ledges to receive presents from The Holy Kings and also to leave a receptacle filled with water for the camels of the Wise Men. In general, Mexico's two Christmases blend into one long holiday period lasting from December 16 to January 6.

In February or March, just before the beginning of Lent, Mexicans celebrate Carnival. These last three to seven days of merry-making before Ash Wednesday, which marks the onset of the six-week Lenten period of penitence and fasting, are a time for street masquerades, fancy-dress balls, and parades with lavish floats. The latter are often sponsored by trade, religious, or other organizations. During Holy Week, the final week of Lent, passion plays are presented and the images of the saints are draped in purple cloth as a sign of deep mourning. On Holy Saturday, the day before Easter Sunday, it is customary to burn a large papier-mâché figure of Judas, the betrayer of Christ. The grotesque Judas is wired with firecrackers and disintegrates in a blaze of fire and a bombardment of noise high above the village square. Easter Sunday, the day of the resurrection of Christ, is once again a time for a joyous fiesta.

Several national holidays also fall during the late-winter and early-spring period. They include Constitution Day on February 5, commemorating the constitutions of 1857 and 1917; Flag Day on February 24, honoring the Mexican flag that was born out of the revolt against Spain in 1821; and the birthday of Benito Juárez on March 21. May 1 is Labor Day, honoring the nation's workers with parades and civic events, while May 5 marks the victory against the French at Puebla in 1862.

The "flying pole dance" performed at El Tajín pyramid
on Corpus Christi Day

A rare spectacle from Mexico's Indian past is revived, oddly
enough, on Corpus Christi Day, a Roman Catholic festival honoring
the body of Christ. This holy day, which falls in late May or early
June, receives special attention on the religious calendar of Spain.
In Mexico, it marks the occasion for El Volador, the "flying pole
dance," which is performed at the pyramid of El Tajín, located
near the town of Papantla in the state of Veracruz. This site was

the home of the Totonacs, a people who dwelt north of the Olmecs, although many centuries later.

Presumably the ritual marked the end of the fifty-two-year Indian "century." The Totonac rite, a form of worship of the sun, began with the climbing of a very high pole placed in the forecourt of the pyramid. According to ancient custom, four *voladores*, or "flyers," ascend the pole, fasten ropes that are connected to the pole around their bodies, and then descend head down, each one making thirteen sweeping revolutions around the pole before reaching the ground. Together the four flyers carry out fifty-two breathtaking turns. The ceremony may have been a gesture of gratitude to the sun-god for a fifty-two-year cycle completed and another one about to begin. At the very top of the pole, a musician is usually perched playing a flute. Elsewhere in Mexico on Corpus Christi Day, infants and children are taken to church to be blessed.

The Mexican autumn brings more national holidays. September 16 is Independence Day. Festivities begin the night before when the Grito de Dolores of Father Hidalgo, first uttered in 1810, once more rings out across the land. As in the United States, October 12 is Columbus Day. Mexicans, however, also call it the Dia de la Raza, Day of the Race, for most owe their heritage to the intermarriage of peoples from the Old World and the New. November 20 is the anniversary of the Revolution of 1910.

Mexicans pay a great deal of attention to the religious festival known as the Day of the Dead, which begins on October 31, Halloween, and continues through November 1, All Saints' Day, and November 2, All Souls' Day. Special cakes and confections appear in bakery windows weeks in advance. Great favorites are skulls made of white sugar and decorated with pink and blue frosting. Also a specialty on this day is *pan de muerto* or "bread of the dead," a dry cake, its rounded surface sprinkled with sugar crystals or spread with sugar icing in the likeness of a skull and crossbones. All-night vigils are held at cemeteries, yellow marigolds (*flores de muerto*) are laid on graves, and in many homes food—perhaps chicken or turkey in mole sauce and pulque—are left out for the visits of departed souls.

Guadalupe Day, in honor of the patron saint of Mexico, is celebrated all over the country on December 12. At the Basilica of

A handicraft tribute to the Day of the Dead
(National Museum of Popular Arts and Industries)

Strolling musicians giving an informal concert
in a church courtyard in Taxco

Guadalupe, the event is marked with folk dances in the great plaza,
as well as religious ceremonies and processions. A few days later,
on December 16, the Christmas *posadas* start to take place, and the
Mexican holiday year with its heavily filled calendar begins anew.

The music and dances that are so vital to Mexico's numerous
festivals are derived partly from Indian forms but show strong
Spanish influence. Very early in the years after the conquest, the
Spanish clergy taught the Indians Spanish dance rituals. One of
them was a stylized reenactment of the struggle between the Moors
and the Christians in fifteenth-century Spain. Although far removed
from the Indian culture of the New World, *moros y cristianos* became firmly entrenched and is even performed at Mexican fiestas
today. The group most responsible for the preservation of Indian
and Indo-Spanish folk dances from all over the country is the Gov-
ernment-sponsored Ballet Folklórico de Mexico. The resident company gives its richly costumed and highly colorful performances at
the Palacio de las Bellas Artes in Mexico City, while touring companies travel both throughout Mexico and internationally.

After the Spanish conquest, the reeds, drums, and conches that provided music for the Indians were gradually replaced by string, percussion, and brass instruments from other parts of the world. A variety of new sounds came into existence, and Mexican music began to develop regional characteristics. Today there are the lushly haunting strains of the mariachi music of Jalisco, performed with guitars, violins, and trumpets; the soft, fluid marimba rhythms of southern Mexico; the *chilena* sounds of west-coast Guerrero state, for which shipwrecked sailors from Chile are believed responsible; and the *veracruzano* music of the east coast, to mention but a few. Both the xylophonelike marimba and the flavor of some of the music of Veracruz state are of African origin. Of the relatively few black slaves that were brought to Mexico, most arrived at the ports of Veracruz and Tampico. As to the word mariachi, it may be traceable to the French *mariage* (marriage), stemming from the French occupation of the 1860's. Actually Spanish in tradition, this music had long been played in Mexico at romantic serenadings and at weddings.

Mariachi music also accompanies the Sunday-afternoon outings of families and groups of friends on rented pleasure boats at the floating gardens of Xochimilco, on the outskirts of Mexico City. Gliding among the merrymakers are boatloads of performing musicians in their silver-studded costumes, as well as smaller craft bearing hawkers of soft drinks, beer, fruit, flowers, and tortillas.

Spanish music is again heard at Mexico's bullfights, which are formally opened with a brassy, flamboyant accompaniment to the entrance of the matadors and other toreros. While the bullfight is considered a spectacle or ritual rather than a sport, Mexicans are also addicted to a number of sports introduced from abroad.

Jai alai is a handball-like game imported from the Basque region of Spain. This fast-moving contest is played on a walled court called a "fronton." The players catch a small, hard ball in a cesta, a wicker basket strapped to the arm, and slam it back against the wall. In professional jai alai betting often runs high and danger is ever present

Boats for hire at the floating gardens of Xochimilco

due to the fury of movement on the court and the almost bulletlike speed of the ball.

Cockfighting was also introduced by the Spanish. Roosters bred for fierceness and power are set against one another in pairs in a pit. Spectators place bets on this bloody fight to the death. Mexico's biggest spectator sport, however, is soccer, as indicated by Mexico City's enormous 105,000-seat Azteca Stadium. Another contemporary sport that deeply absorbs Mexicans is *beisbol*, a popular import from the United States. World attention focused on Mexican achievements in sports when, in 1968, Mexico City played host to the Olympic Games.

Indian skills and artistry plus Spanish materials and techniques blend with particularly happy results in the handicrafts of Mexico, which are among the most varied and creative in the world. The Indians of pre-Hispanic times were masters at working gold and silver and cutting gemstones, at weaving and dyeing reeds and grasses as well as cotton, at featherwork and pottery making. The Spanish added materials like wrought iron, leather, wool, glass, ceramic tiles, and new dyes to supplement the colorings used by the Indians, which were extracted from various plants and insects. Gradually local craft specialties developed in different parts of the country. To this day, most articles are made in homes or workshops where the individual craftsperson has control of the object being fashioned from start to finish, and assembly-line processes are scorned.

Among regional specialties, Jalisco is known for its hand-tooled leather goods and blown glass, the state of Michoacán for its trays

Black pottery and other ceramics crafted in Oaxaca

Rich Spanish baroque altar of Church of Santo Domingo in Oaxaca, built in colonial era

and boxes of lacquerware, the state of Tlaxcala for its woolen serapes and rebozos, Taxco for its jewelry and other objects of silver, Oaxaca for its black pottery, and Puebla for its glazed blue-and-white pottery of Moorish-Spanish inspiration. Hand-embroidered shirts, blouses, and other fine fabrics are made in the Yucatán, while woven baskets and other straw goods are found at markets almost everywhere.

Throughout the colonial era, religious architecture had been Mexico's major art form. The nineteenth century, particularly the period of Porfirio Díaz, saw Mexican artists going to Europe to study and wealthy Mexicans importing the work of Europeans. But the Revolution of 1910 was the inspiration for a new school of art that was purely Mexican, drawing strongly on Indian, folk, and patriotic themes and expressing itself in massive murals often presented as frescoes applied to the plaster walls of modern buildings.

Mexico's public art, bold in its condemnation of historical and social injustices and fierce with pride in the national culture, was produced in large part by the revolutionary painters, Diego Rivera (1886–1957) and David Alfaro Siqueiros (1896–1974). A third muralist, less the political propagandist but intensely compassionate in his view of human suffering, was José Clemente Orozco (1883–1949). The idea of using art as propaganda originated with a militant figure of the Porfirio Díaz era, the artist Gerardo Murillo, better known as Dr. Atl (1877–1964). (*Atl* is the Aztec word for water.) Another prominent Mexican painter of the twentieth century is Rufino Tamayo, born in 1899. While not a muralist or a propagandist, he has transmitted deep feeling for the plight of the Indian in his work and has introduced more flexibility of style into Mexican painting. He is also a brilliant colorist.

Mexico's literary tradition goes back to the chronicles, histories, and tracts of the Indians and of the Spanish explorers and clergy in the early Hispanic era. The Mayans produced the Biblelike *Popol Vuh*, a saga of the creation of the world that also set forth Mayan religious thought. It was written shortly after the conquest of the Yucatán, in the Mayan Quiché language but with Latin characters, and was translated into several languages including English. Other postconquest Indian writings that have been translated are the Books of Chilam Balam, a Mayan priest. They contain material on history, medicine, religion, and astrology.

Among the first Spaniards to set foot in New Spain was Bernal

Dr. Atl, Mexican revolutionist, painter,
and originator of propagandist mural art

Díaz del Castillo, a member of the expeditions of 1517 and 1518 as
well as Cortés' expedition of 1519. His eyewitness account, *The True
History of the Conquest of New Spain*, set down in his later years,
was a fascinating and richly detailed piece of reporting, written
with warmth and spontaneity. Cortés, too, wrote abundantly, mainly
in a long series of dispatches to the king of Spain, which began
while the campaign for conquest was still going on. The writings of

the Spanish priest, Bartolomé de las Casas, were pleas for more humane and enlightened treatment of the Indians, while Father Bernardino de Sahagún and others wrote careful and systematic descriptions of Indian life and culture.

In recent times Mexico's writers, like its artists, have been deeply concerned with the nature and the complex problems of Mexican society. Among the most probing and analytical writers of the twentieth century have been the poet and essayist, Octavio Paz, born in 1914, and the novelist Carlos Fuentes, born in 1929. Interestingly enough, both men have served in the Government as foreign ambassadors.

In *The Labyrinth of Solitude*, essays written in 1950, Paz sees the Mexican as troubled and defensive, seeking pride and honor but haunted by the cruelties of the Aztec past and the violations of the Spanish conquest. The Mexican man, in particular, seeks to heal the injuries to his spirit and to attain a strong, personal identity by taking on the quality of *machismo*. The person who would be *macho* takes action with an attitude of indifference to the consequences and exercises his power over others lest they, like his former masters, use theirs to subdue him. Paz unhappily sees his countrymen condemned to a continuing condition of anguish, for most are caught in a social and economic structure that locks them into poverty and subservience.

Carlos Fuentes, whose work has been widely translated, published his first and very well-received novel, *La region más transparente* (*Where the Air Is Clear*), in 1958. His most recent novel, *Terra Nostra* (*Our Land*), appeared in 1976. Fuentes deplores the failure of Mexico's revolutions to achieve widespread social betterment and stability. Instead he feels that they have nurtured new classes of privilege and wealth and that the heroes of the revolutionary movements were themselves inevitably corrupted by success, unless they died while the process of change was still in progress. In Fuentes' novels, Mexican society is portrayed as chaotic and its people disoriented. Like Paz, he is a sharp critic of the social and economic conditions of contemporary Mexico.

Indeed, beneath the color, contrasts, and endless fascination of the land of three cultures run the more somber threads of everyday life. Whether in the remote farming villages or on the bustling urban scene, the problems of the landless, the homeless, the victims of poverty, illiteracy, and social indifference persist. The dreams of the Revolution of 1910, and of the uprisings and reform movements that preceded it, have not yet become a reality.

4 Village Life, City Life

On the tourist-traveled route through Mexico, the casual visitor sees almost nothing of everyday life. The traveler who arrives by air is usually set down in or near Mexico City's Zona Rosa (Pink Zone) with its sleek hotels and elegant shops, is then whisked off to Taxco with its storybook cobbled streets and well-stocked jewelry shops, and at last deposited on the glittering sands of Acapulco. The nearly half of the Mexican population that lives in rural or semirural backwaters, the 50 percent or more that is unemployed or underemployed, is fleetingly glimpsed at most. Nor are the poverty *vecindades* (neighborhoods), and packing-crate squatters' camps that surround and blotch the capital and other large cities ever explored.

Today many of Mexico's poor families are in a state of transition, moving from remote primitive communities toward urban centers. They exchange candlelight or kerosene lamps for electricity, charcoal cooking fires for three-burner gas stoves, bare feet or huaraches (their soles often cut from old rubber tires) for shoes. But the quality of their lives does not necessarily improve. Poverty bred of social inequalities and economic ills, lack of education and opportunity, overpopulation, ignorance, and superstition moves with them from the countryside to the city.

Close to 40 percent of Mexico's families are rural and survive mainly by farming. The fields they work may belong to a landowner, may be communally owned, or may be wholly their own. Corn and beans are the staple crops that sustain the family and, if there is a surplus, can be sold or bartered for additional foodstuffs, clothing,

or other basic needs. But, because of the primitive agricultural methods used, harvests are usually skimpy and daily existence is apt to be hand-to-mouth. Those who are hired out as farm laborers are generally no better off, for most are paid peon's wages and are usually deeply in debt, forfeiting tomorrow's money for today's subsistence.

One of the goals of the Revolution of 1910 was to break the power of the wealthy landowners and redistribute their holdings to the peasants. Although millions of acres were taken from the rich in the years following the Revolution, nearly half of Mexico's farming population of about twenty-five million is today either landless (about four million) or on the brink of starvation because of the low productivity of tiny plots.

Much of the land redistributed in accordance with the constitution of 1917 was assigned to the *ejido* system rather than given outright to individual peasants. *Ejido* lands are owned by the community and are worked on a cooperative basis by the local villagers. The term is derived from the word *exit*, for these fields are usually located just outside the villages. The idea of communal farming has much in common with the systems used in pre-Hispanic times. It was thought that the *ejidos* would prove a success, as the villages would be better able to qualify for agricultural loans for farming equipment, fertilizer, seed, animal feed, and so forth than would the individual farmers. A National Ejidal Credit Bank was established and *ejido* marketing cooperatives formed, and an effort was made to bring social services, schools, and complete rural development programs to the *ejido* villages.

On the whole, the *ejido* system has been less than successful. The 70 percent of the rural population that works on *ejido* lands pro-

Opposite, top: A village dwelling in the state of Hidalgo
Bottom: A poverty quarter in Acapulco just behind a lavish resort hotel

Members of a Lake Pátzcuaro village cooperative
that has purchased chicken feed on credit

duces only 35 percent of Mexico's total farm output. Many of the
lands given over to the peasantry were of marginal quality, with
overworked and depleted soil and lacking adequate rainfall or irrigation facilities. Many of the villages were either too poor to qualify
for adequate agricultural assistance or were inefficient in utilizing
the assistance they got. Unable to reap sufficient food from the *ejido*

lands, the peasants began to abandon them or to seek part-time work elsewhere. In addition, the Government's enthusiasm for the *ejido* concept varied from one presidential administration to another, and, in many cases, enterprising financial interests illegally took over *ejido* lands, obtained credit loans to make them productive, and then began hiring the local peasants to work on them for low wages.

As the burden of feeding Mexico's growing urban population has increased with each year, Government authorities have tended to ignore such artful business maneuvers. Similarly, many large private farming estates have reemerged, despite laws that limit the maximum acreage of such property. Not only are well-financed, mechanized farms better able to grow food for Mexico's people, but, in the case of the vast agro-industrial enterprises of Mexico's northwestern states, they also grow food for export to the United States.

Luis Echeverría Alvarez, president of Mexico from 1970 to 1976, frequently gave strong verbal support to the plight of the landless and hungry peasants, assuring them that they would yet see the goals of the 1910 Revolution fulfilled. A few weeks before he left office in December 1976 to make way for his elected successor, Echeverría ordered the expropriation of over 200,000 acres of farmland in Sonora state, for redistribution to landless peasants. His action spurred peasant sit-ins on large private farms in neighboring Sinaloa state (which grows about 40 percent of the winter vegetables consumed in the United States).

Soon after Echeverría was out of power, however, a federal judge revoked the order, which seemed like little more than the hollow gesture of a leader seeking to leave office on a popular note. As in numerous other cases of land occupation in recent years, the groups of angry peasants were no match for the powerful landowners allied with big-business interests, and eventually they were evicted with Government cooperation.

From a practical point of view, there would not be any real advantage in turning over Mexico's developed and profitable farms to impoverished and unskilled peasant owners. The national economy is highly dependent on the benefits derived from this commercially successful agricultural sector. Mexico's current president, José López Portillo, believes that there has been "too much faith placed in the redistribution of land as a means of solving inequalities" and that the time for such remedies is long past. "What the peasant really seeks through land possession," López Portillo says, "is security of employment and income. There are other ways of offering that kind of security."

Meantime, life continues in the old way in the Mexican hinterlands. Villages nestled on the higher slopes of the Sierra Madres may be so distant from the nearest paved road that they are accessible only by donkey trail or by helicopter. They lack electricity, a reliable water supply, or sanitary facilities of any kind. Houses built of adobe brick (blocks of sunbaked mud and straw) or other local materials often consist of one windowless room in which an entire family, with numerous children and often grandparents and other relatives, sleeps, eats, and performs its daily chores.

The tortilla is still the staple food of the rural family, although bread made of wheat flour or a sweet roll may be obtained occasionally. Most communities now have mills that grind corn into masa for making tortillas. But the women have kept their metates and often rework the mill-ground, soaked corn to give it the "taste of the stone." When times are hard, even the small cost of having corn ground at the mill may be too much to spend, and the woman of the house returns to the laborious task of grinding corn into masa by hand.

The day begins before dawn with the shaping and toasting of the tortillas that the men will take to the fields for their noon dinner, as many as twenty-five per person, along with a homemade sauce of chilies and a clay jug of home-brewed tea or other beverage. The foods eaten at breakfast, dinner, and supper are almost completely interchangeable. In addition to tortillas three times a day, there may be rice, beans, squash or another local vegetable, home-grown fruit, and coffee. Peasant families may keep chickens or turkeys but will sell or trade the eggs and the birds for necessities like cooking fuel, kerosene, clothing and household articles, and other manufactured items that they cannot supply themselves. Eggs, poultry, and meat tend to be rarities on the peasant table.

The cheapest of all commodities is human labor. Many pairs of hands are needed in the family, for working the fields, hauling firewood and well water, preparing food, cleaning and tidying the cramped living quarters to keep them habitable, weaving rope and cloth, and performing countless other daily tasks and errands. So Mexican families are large. Although infant and child mortality rates on a national scale are declining, poor families still frequently experience the deaths of offspring from malnutrition and disease and feel that the more children one has the greater the guarantee of helping hands and security in one's old age. Many rural and also city families ignore medical facilities and prefer to bring their sick to *curanderos*, so-called healers whose "remedies" are culled from a mixture of Indian practices, spiritualism, and folk medicines and superstitions. Most major killers like smallpox, malaria, typhus, and yellow fever have, however, been virtually wiped out in Mexico.

Today, with its death rate dropping and its average life-span extending into the late sixties, Mexico has one of the highest rates of population growth in the world. In the twenty-year period between 1957 and 1977, the country's population more than doubled, increasing from thirty million to sixty-three million. And, at its current rate of growth, the population will nearly double to one hundred fifteen million by the year 2000.

In the past twenty years, Mexico City's population grew from four million to a stifling ten million (twelve million if the fringe metropolitan area is included, as it must be). Even higher urban growth rates have taken place in Mexico's next-to-largest cities, Guadalajara and Monterrey, during that time span. The forecast for

Mexico City in the year 2000 is an almost unbelievable thirty million, for the population of the cities is growing at a faster rate than it is for the country as a whole. Already more than 60 percent of the Mexican people are city dwellers rather than country dwellers.

The Government's introduction, in 1973, of birth-control programs on the note of "responsible parenthood" has brought births down

Children from the families of the poor,
part of Mexico's huge youth population

only slightly thus far (to a growth rate of 3.2 percent, as opposed to a world average of 1.9 percent and a United States rate of .9 percent). Thus, the makings of an explosive situation are still present. Seventy percent of Mexico's people are under the age of twenty-five and have the potential for high fertility in the years ahead. The hazards for an overpopulated and impoverished nation include massive unemployment, crime, the lowering of living standards for the poorer classes, and the deterioration of the quality of life for all. Yet traditional institutions and the religious beliefs of many Mexicans seem to run counter to President López Portillo's plea for responsible family planning in his watchword slogan, *la solución somos todos*, "the solution is all of us."

Unable to keep their families fed and seeing no possibility of betterment in their primitive and neglected villages, peasants move to the cities, often arriving barefoot and carrying their possessions on their backs. Their first stop may be a squatters' camp on the outskirts, in a dwelling patched together out of cardboard and scraps of wood and metal. Once jobs are found by some of the family members, they may move into a one- or two-room tenement apartment in one of the many slum *vecindades*, usually rows of cement single-story units with a common patio or courtyard and an outdoor toilet facility and water pump that must be shared by a number of families. In the better *vecindades*, there may be an indoor toilet for each apartment as well as electricity and running water.

The attractions of city living soon tempt the family into making extra expenditures, undreamed of back in the village. Tortillas can be purchased ready-to-eat at the *tortillería*, usually a corner shop to which children are sent on errands for a fresh supply for each meal. Fancy breads and rolls, snack foods and ice cream, and all sorts of candies and sweets also wean away the pesos, as do bus fares, movies, *discotecas*, and the beers and alcoholic drinks that are soon preferred over pulque.

The presence of numerous neighbors not only intrudes on the family's privacy but engages it in both a daily and long-range competition to "keep up with the Joneses." Tortillas and spoons as eating utensils give way to the more sophisticated forks and knives; aluminum cooking pots are purchased and the clay vessels of the country-

Town dwellers wearing store-bought trousers and shoes;
calzones and huaraches would be the equivalent for country folk

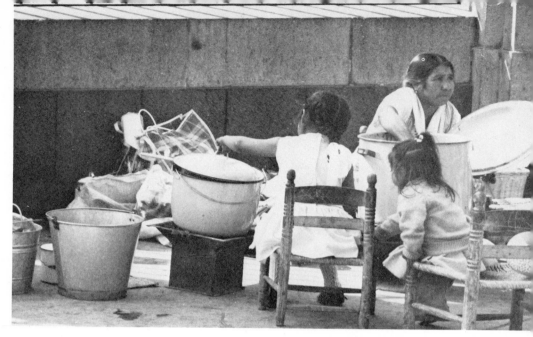

A sidewalk vendor of home-cooked food accompanied by her children

side are gradually put aside. Store-bought trousers replace the pajamalike, white *calzones* of the men and boys, and the entire family needs shoes to wear on the city streets. Soon a radio, a bicycle, some items of furniture, and perhaps a sewing machine are purchased. The family's indebtedness for consumer goods grows with each acquisition. If possible, they borrow against their salaries or from each other or from their neighbors. They pawn certain items to try to keep up the payments on other items, seek additional income by sending out younger family members to become street vendors or to live by their wits. But their debts continue to mount, particularly if illness or other misfortune strikes. Most poor city dwellers become caught up in a cycle of defeat; nevertheless, they continue to be lured by the prospect of one day owning a television set, a washing machine, a refrigerator, even an automobile.

The family itself takes on a different character as it becomes acclimated to city life. The children grow freer in their manners and less respectful toward their elders. Boys and young men who once obediently farmed the land alongside their fathers find jobs that

take them away from home each day, into the diversified activities
of the city. Petty criminal activity lurks everywhere. For thieves
and pickpockets work the streets, the markets, and especially the
buses, just as in other teeming cities in most parts of the world. And
the temptation to obtain goods or money easily can be overpower-
ing. Girls, once given a taste of the urban scene, tend to discard
the family-inculcated roles of modesty and passivity and to be bolder
in their relationships with the opposite sex, more eager for attractive
clothes and cosmetics, parties and dances.

The position of the woman in Mexican society has been dual in
nature. Submissive and subservient to her husband, she is at the
same time an authoritarian figure to her children. Even her sons,
when grown, may find themselves dominating their own wives but
still obedient and adoring toward their mothers. The heavy household, barnyard, and child-rearing chores of the rural woman do not
necessarily grow lighter with the move to the city. Although she
may be able to buy certain precooked foods and to obtain a few
simple home conveniences, she still carries a daily burden of house-
work and caring for others and, in addition, may try to help meet
the family's debts by going out to peddle cheap goods or trinkets.
Or she may prepare tortillas, chicken mole, or sweets at home, which
she will try to sell in the streets.

The woman's responsibility for her family further increases in the
city setting due to the high rate of desertion. It is estimated that a
third or more of all unions, particularly among the poorer classes,
are common-law marriages. Even legally married men often consider themselves free to take on other "wives" in what is known as
free union, for doing so is an evidence of *machismo*. Some work
hard attempting to maintain two or more households and to care
for the children of the various unions. But should the male parent
desert the family unit, the burden of supporting and caring for the
children falls wholly on the mother, reinforcing the matriarchal
aspects of Mexican family life.

Female proprietors of stands selling religious pictures and jewelry
near the Shrine of Guadalupe

Because the children of the poor are able to earn a few pesos
working as helpers or messengers in the manual trades or for small
businesses, they are often kept out of the primary school grades.
Education is compulsory through the sixth grade or to age fourteen,
whichever comes first, but the majority of children do not attend
regularly and most do not complete all six years. Poor parents reason
that two or three years of schooling will not guarantee a better job,
and keeping a child in school until graduation often requires too
many sacrifices. Poor city families still believe, as rural ones usually
have, that children should be economic assets from an early age.
They see nothing wrong in encouraging a nine-year-old to earn a
little money to help out.

Although Mexico's literacy rate has been climbing (from close
to zero at the end of the colonial period and only 15 to 20 percent
in 1910), it is estimated that 38 percent of the population is still
unable to read and write. Among the remaining 62 percent there
are many with extremely limited skills who should probably be
classified as semiliterate at best. Some observers consider only 50

percent of the population to be in possession of a meaningful degree of literacy.

Public education started late in Mexico. The first schools after the conquest were, of course, missionary taught. The Franciscan friars were the earliest to arrive and built a mission school and church, along with a monastery and hospital, in Mexico City in 1524. In addition to religion, the Indian students learned Spanish and a little Latin, crafts, and music. The Royal and Pontifical University of Mexico was chartered in 1551. Its purpose was to educate the sons of the wealthy Spanish colonists. All courses were taught in Latin and the main areas of study were theology, medicine, and classical literature.

Not until some years after the Revolution of 1910 did "cultural missions" begin to be trained, much like the religious missions of an earlier day, to go out into the countryside armed with some knowledge of Indian customs and languages. Their purpose was to teach not only reading and writing, but the rudiments of modern sanitation and hygiene, and skills in carpentry, masonry, forging, and agriculture that would be immediate and useful to the lives of the semiprimitive rural population. In addition, this type of schooling was important for implanting the goals of the Revolution and instilling pride in the national heritage. Popular drives for mass schooling and literacy got under way in the 1940's when President Manuel Ávila Camacho decreed that every Mexican who knew how to read and write should teach at least one other Mexican to do so.

In 1955, the University City campus near the outskirts of Mexico City was dedicated, and the National Autonomous University of Mexico soon became housed in its strikingly designed, mosaic-walled buildings. A very different institution from the Royal and Pontifical of the colonial era, the National University offered a broad program of study and considered itself not only independent of state interference but a tool of conscience for criticizing and influencing Government policy.

Student activists came to the fore in Mexico City's university demonstrations of 1968, a time of similar protests in many parts of the world. Although the Mexican demonstrations calling for political and economic reforms, changes in the penal code, and an end to Government corruption were peaceful, they met with severe repressive measures. About 200 students were killed and many more jailed. The fact that the protests took place at about the time that Mexico City was playing host to the Olympic Games may have accounted in part for the Government's overreaction.

Responsibility for the student deaths appeared to rest with the then president, Gustavo Díaz Ordaz, and his minister of the interior, Luis Echeverría Alvarez, who, in 1970, became president of Mexico. As president, Echeverría gave in to some student demands while suppressing the activities of the more radical groups. His principal

Mosaic facade of the library building at the National University designed by architect Juan O'Gorman

tactics of appeasement seem to have been the appointment of some graduates to high Government posts and also the enlargement of the entire university system, which operates a number of state universities throughout Mexico. Between 1970 and 1976, the total national enrollment doubled to over 500,000.

Unfortunately, the academic quality of the student bodies and of the teaching appears to have dropped through Echeverría's broad admissions policy. And the undercurrents of strife have not vanished. Mexico's universities may well become a major testing ground for the political struggle between the country's rightist and leftist elements.

In today's Mexico, the barriers that once stratified society into classes are fast disappearing. From early colonial times, the principal social distinction was between those who performed manual labor and those who did not. At the very peak of the social structure were the *flor y nata*, "flower and cream," of affluent landowners and top Government and church officials. On lower levels, but still on the favored side of the manual-labor barrier, were doctors, lawyers, owners of prosperous businesses, smaller private landowners, the clergy, educators of higher rank, and clerks in the upper echelons. On the opposite side of the dividing line was all the rest of society: agricultural workers, craftsmen and artisans, laborers, servants, peddlers, even police and primary-school teachers. Beggers, *pepenadores* (those who live by scrounging in refuse dumps), drunkards, and the indigent were at the very bottom of the social heap. And it would not have been a simple matter for an Indian or a mestizo who somehow had managed to strike it rich to cross into the upper ranks of society.

Nowadays, however, the question of how one earns one's money is no longer so important as how much one earns, and a manual worker from village or city may manage to leap from poverty to affluence with all its trappings. While it does not happen often, a combination of shrewdness, luck, and tenacity can sometimes work such a miracle. More often, upward mobility is achieved by steps: the sole educated member of a poor family becomes a civil servant or small business entrepreneur; a son carries the family on through Mexico's emerging middle class, or a well-bred and reasonably well-educated daughter marries into a wealthy family, either established in its position or newly rich.

As soon as a Mexican family becomes well-to-do it tends to adopt the life-styles and consumer goods of the United States. A home in Chapultepec Heights or in the Pedregal residential district of Mexico City resembles a comfortable-to-opulent American subur-ban home in its furnishings, carpeting, labor-saving devices, stereo and television sets. In addition, the Mexican family is sure to have servants, probably a cook and a housemaid at the very least. Typi-cally, the servants "live in," occupying quarters on the flat roof of the house.

Advertising and investment in Mexico, movies, television, and tourism, have made Mexicans highly responsive to brand names and products from the United States. In the larger cities, many

At the delicatessen counter of an American-style supermarket in Cuernavaca

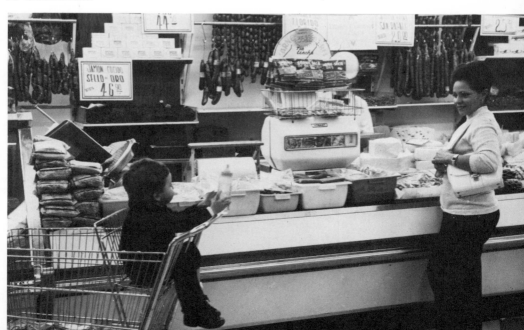

Exploring the features of supermarket shopping,
so different from the Indian and peasant markets

imported goods or close imitations can be purchased in branches
of well-known United States' retail chains or in supermarkets styled
like those in the United States. All along the border from Texas to
California, towns on the United States side have become merchan-
dise meccas for prosperous and enterprising Mexicans who want
to stock up on everything from detergents and powdered soft
drinks to expensive watches and designer-label clothing. Although
border crossings like that between the shoppers' paradise of Laredo,
Texas, and the town of Nuevo Laredo, Mexico, are heavily staffed
with customs inspectors, the low-paid Mexican officials are often
susceptible when offered the customary *mordida,* or bribe.

In the prosperous Mexican household, the day usually begins
with a servant-prepared breakfast of juice, cereal, and/or bacon-
and-eggs, pancakes with syrup, toast with marmalade, and coffee.
Tortillas, beans, and chili are relegated to the past, or to the servants
should they prefer them. Other meals are also similar to those north
of the border. The man of the house may return home from his
office for a main meal at midday, but more and more city dwellers
of some means prefer the snack and sandwich bars and fast-service
restaurants that have sprung up.

Fads and fashions from north of the border are quickly adopted by the most affluent families. They, in turn, are carefully watched by the less affluent for the latest trends, whether in household furnishings and gadgets, men's and women's clothing, children's toys and comic books, or other status symbols. Beginning in 1976, the infatuation in the United States with citizen's-band radios crossed the border and was taken up by the youth of well-to-do families. And the vogue for having an evergreen tree decorated with glittering ornaments and colored lights at Christmas time has become a "must" for all those who can afford one.

Although the upper-class Mexican woman has material goods and physical comforts far beyond the reach of her poorer sisters, she often finds her subservient role harder to escape. As she is well provided for, there is seldom any justification for her getting a job or having a career of her own. Such an activity might well be viewed as a poor reflection on her husband's earning ability and a slur on his *machismo*. Her days are usually taken up with giving orders to the servants and with a round of shopping and card-playing activities. This situation is now on the brink of changing. Recent presidential addresses have called for expanded opportunities for women and for the equalization of pay scales between the sexes. Already younger married women have begun to pursue jobs outside the home and to aspire to business and professional careers.

The children of the wealthy are often coddled and may be less respectful to their parents than the children of the poor. The father, however, tends to wield the most power, largely because of his exclusive control of the purse strings. If the family is nouveau riche, the parents may frequently overcompensate, showering the young ones with costly clothes, toys, sports and recreation equipment, and special treats in an effort to give them the things they never had when young. Meantime, the real values of family life—understanding, affection, shared activities—may be overlooked.

Among Mexico's families of established wealth, there are still many *criollos*, fair-skinned and with non-Indian features, who can trace their ancestry back to sixteenth-century Spain. President José López Portillo is of such a background. Mestizos, of course, make up an increasing proportion of Mexico's middle class and more recently well-to-do families. But despite the many public and cultural expressions of national pride in the country's Indian heritage, there is no question that differences in skin color are recognized. Par-

Girls from well-to-do Mexican families,
the two on the right wearing school uniforms

A political poster
("Our children are the inheritors of the Revolution")
portraying a woman of *criollo* rather than mestizo appearance

ticularly in the selection of marriage partners, fairer-skinned people are preferred.

Even among the Indian and mestizo poor, parents will sometimes shield their lighter-skinned offspring from the sun to prevent their complexions from darkening. Many of the faces shown on advertising posters and billboards in Mexico are distinctly non-Indian. This preference may be a reflection not only of the colonial past but of what some observers see as Mexico's national habit of comparing itself unfavorably with the United States.

Two major causes of friction between the two countries in recent years are the large quantities of drugs and the ever-growing number of illegal migrant workers crossing the border from Mexico into the United States. Both problems are, of course, related to Mexico's widespread poverty and grave unemployment situation. The per capita income for Mexicans is presently only $740 a year (only $175 for the average rural worker), and the rate of inflation has recently run as high as 30 percent. Social-security benefits are available only to those who work at Government jobs and in certain private-business sectors of the economy. Many workers in marginal and agricultural employment have no coverage at all. They receive no sick benefits, unemployment-insurance payments, or retirement pension, and general welfare services to assist the needy are spotty at best. The new high-rise housing developments that dot the city skylines are mainly for civil servants and other middle-income families. So it is not suprising that a business as lucrative as the traffic in illegal drugs should attract a number of Mexicans.

The principal marijuana and opium-poppy fields are located in a V-shaped sector of northern Mexico. The southerly apex of the drug belt is in the state of Durango, with its network fanning out northward to towns all along the 2000-mile border with the United States. A peasant who grows two or three acres of opium poppies, reaping two or possibly three harvests a year, can earn as much as $4000 annually, a relatively huge amount of money. The plantings are usually hidden in rough, highly inaccessible country, on fields the peasant does not own, often on Government land. Once the poppy flower loses its red petals, small cuts are made in the naked seedpod. By the following day, the opium gum has seeped out and is collected by the farmer. It is then picked up for transportation to towns like Culiacán and Durango, where it is processed into "Mexican brown," a semirefined form of heroin. The Mexican product is not as pure and not as reduced in volume as the white variety, such as that manufactured in France from Turkish-grown poppies.

For smuggling across the border, Mexican heroin and marijuana are concealed in trucks, automobiles, light airplanes, even on the bodies of women and children slipping through at both official crossing points and at unsupervised stretches, such as places along the Rio Grande. Most of the heroin is then transported to Chicago, which is a major reprocessing and redistribution center.

As about 80 percent of the heroin found in the United States today is Mexican grown, both Mexican and United States narcotics agencies have stepped up their efforts at detection and policing. They have even tried using herbicides sprayed from helicopters to kill the plants and thus snuff out the trade at the source. But it is estimated that there are some 20,000 tiny plots of opium poppies scattered through the drug-growing belt. The peasants responsible for their cultivation, who receive only a pittance compared with the overall take, seldom even see the faces of the middlemen who surreptitiously pick up the raw opium gum and leave the payment. The traffic itself is run by sophisticated and dangerous elements that make the job of the Mexican *federales* both difficult and hazardous.

Repeatedly United States authorities have criticized the Mexican drug agents for not being more efficient, while the Mexicans have charged the Americans with laxity in effectively prosecuting drug traffickers and drug users in the United States. On the Mexican side of the border, the authorities have been firm in their treatment of such individuals, remanding both Mexican citizens and foreigners to prison on drug charges and keeping them there for long periods while awaiting trial. Mexico does not at present have a severe heroin-user problem. But marijuana, long employed by the rural poor as a cheap substitute for alcohol, is now said to be available at most schools and universities. This development appears traceable to United States influence, stemming from the late 1960's when the use of drugs peaked among students and youth.

Probably the most far-reaching effect of the United States on Mexicans is the lure of a better life. The poor Mexican must work for weeks, perhaps months, to earn the sum that a middle-class American spends for one night in an Acapulco hotel room. This is but one of the many glaring examples of economic disparity between the two countries that the Mexican sees.

Between 1951 and 1964, the United States permitted braceros,

A soft-drink advertisement from the United States, one of the many
influences that may one day lure this Oaxaca child north

Mexican field workers, to migrate seasonally into the country, re-
turning to Mexico with earnings much higher than those possible
at home. Today, because of the pressure of American labor organizations, no such agreement exists. But, with at least a third of
the Mexican labor force unemployed and many more only margin-
ally employed, it is not surprising that several thousand Mexicans

emigrate to the United States illegally each day. Once in California or one of the other Southwestern states, the Mexican finds that he can earn five to seven times as much as he can in Mexico.

Illegal entry is a tricky and dangerous business. Evading the border guards is only part of the problem. To do so, the would-be immigrants must choose desolate stretches of country or must swim the Rio Grande. The latter method of entry has earned them the name of wetbacks. Many illegals are met, by prearrangement, by *polleros*, "chicken herders," who escort them into the United States and deposit them in a town or city for sums ranging from $50 to $200. Others, attempting to find their way on their own, are frequently set upon by brutal gangs, both Mexican and American, operating on both sides of the border. Entire families may be robbed of their money and possessions and often subjected to physical violence. They are unable to lodge complaints with either the Mexican or American authorities, for they themselves are in violation of the law.

Despite these risks and difficulties, illegal aliens continue to flow into the United States, where they find jobs as migrant agricultural workers, on construction crews, and at other kinds of manual labor. Usually they work under hiring bosses and always for wages that are below scale. Like the drug trade, the tide of illegal immigration goes unchecked as long as there is a profit to be wrung from it. United States employers and contractors are willing to fill labor quotas with low-paid aliens rather than with citizens or other legal residents to whom they would have to pay standard rates. The impoverished Mexicans are too desperate to be concerned about principles of morality and fair labor practices.

It is estimated that at present more than half of the six to eight million illegal aliens in the United States are Mexicans. Although large numbers of would-be entrants are apprehended at the border, three or four probably slip through for every one that is caught and turned back. Of all the Hispanic peoples of the Americas currently entering the United States, Mexicans make up the overwhelming majority. Most settle permanently in California, Arizona, New Mexico, Texas, and Colorado, which contain about 60 percent of the United States population of Mexican origin. Recently more and more Mexicans have been filtering north into the Great Lakes area and particularly Chicago. Not all Mexicans, of course, are illegal aliens; many have entered the country under the laws of immigration.

However, the influx of illegals is not only likely to continue at the current rate of one million per year but to grow even larger as long as Mexico is plagued with rapid population growth, massive unemployment, and erosive inflation. These conditions, the root of many troubles, pose serious problems for the Mexican Government, not only internally but in its relations with its powerful and influential neighbor to the north and in its position on the international scene.

5 Mexico on the World Scene

A first glance at Mexico's political structure and economic system is apt to be highly confusing. Is the Mexican Government a democracy or a dictatorship? Is it revolutionary or repressive? Is the country's economy socialist or capitalist? Just as Mexico's culture and population are a blend of disparate elements, so its political and economic characteristics seem to be made up of a mass of contradictions.

Consider Mexico's federal system of government. In many ways it appears to resemble closely that of the United States. The country, officially known as Estados Unidos Mexicanos (United Mexican States), is divided into thirty-one states plus the Distrito Federal, or Federal District, in which Mexico City, the national capital, is located. Like Washington, D.C., Mexico D.F. is also the seat of government of its own small enclave, the Federal District. The capital is most often referred to inside the country simply as Mexico, while outsiders know it as Mexico City. Sometimes additional confusion is caused by the fact that one of the thirty-one states is also named Mexico (México in Spanish), just as the United States has a state named Washington. The capital of the state of Mexico is Toluca.

Like its neighbor to the north, Mexico has a two-house congress: a senate, with two senators elected from each state and from the Federal District, and a chamber of deputies, with over 200 representatives elected from voting districts all over the country. Mexicans of eighteen and over enjoy universal suffrage, regardless of

The capital's 44-story Latin-American Tower, its tallest building

literacy, and vote freely in all elections. Women received the vote
for the first time in 1955. The constitution guarantees freedom of
speech and places no restriction on the freedom to form political
parties.

Yes, despite all these indications of democracy, Mexico is essen-
tially a single-party state, the president may run for office un-

opposed, the states have little autonomy, and the congress has no veto power. It cannot effectively check the authority of the chief executive, who holds the reins of government for six years and runs the country virtually single-handed. The president, in fact, has such broad powers that some observers have called his term in office a "six-year dictatorship." How did this state of affairs come about and how has it managed to survive in such an orderly fashion ever since the inauguration of President Lázaro Cárdenas in 1934?

La república, as Mexicans call it, has been in the grip of the Partido Revolucionario Institucional (PRI), or Institutional Revolu-

Mexican women voting in their first presidential election in 1958

tionary Party, ever since the formation of that body in 1929. The party's founders intended it to serve as a broad-based power center, embodying the ideals of the Revolution of 1910 and, at the same time, working to preserve the system and its institutions as established at the close of the revolutionary period. The PRI is flexible but only within limits, for its purpose is to guard against giving Mexico more democracy than it can handle and to prevent any threats to the nation's stability from either the left or the right. Compared to other countries of Latin America, with their frequent and bloody coups, military dictatorships, and radical swings and reverses in political philosophy, Mexico has weathered the most vol-

PRI posters popularizing the presidential candidate for 1976, José López Portillo

atile decades of the twentieth century with remarkable steadiness.

Perhaps, as inheritors of the pre-Hispanic ideal of reverence and loyalty toward absolute rulers, Mexicans can more readily accept the idea of an absolute president than could citizens of some of the Western democracies. While it is true that the Mexican president is barred from reelection after his six-year term, he has the exclusive option of choosing his successor while still in office. He thus perpetuates the system of which he is a part. His choice, at first, is secret and is identified only as the *tapado*, "concealed one." Later his name will become well known and he will tour the country, campaigning as though he were one of several serious contenders. But as the candidate of the PRI he is assured victory. The role of the electorate will be merely to approve the departing president's choice.

As its constitution guarantees, Mexico does have other political parties: the conservative, right-wing PAN (Partido de Acción Nacional, or National Action Party); the left-wing PPS (Partido Popular Socialista, or Popular Socialist Party); and the PARM (Partido Auténtico de la Revolucíon Mexicaña, or Authentic Party of the Mexican Revolution), which advocates a stricter return to revolutionary goals. There is a Mexican Communist Party, which, along with several other extreme leftist groups, is still in the process of seeking full legal recognition.

Although the smaller recognized parties do elect candidates to the federal chamber of deputies and to some state and local offices, the PRI has put every president, federal senator, and state governor into office since 1929. In the presidential election of July 4, 1976 (the first Sunday in July is Election Day in Mexico), the PPS and the PARM supported José López Portillo and the PAN did not choose to put forward any candidate. So, for the first time since 1929, the voters were not given a choice of even one minority-party candidate. (In the 1970 election, Luis Echeverría Alvarez drew nearly 12,000,000 votes against the minority candidate's 1,900,000.)

Luis Echeverría Alvarez, controversial president of Mexico from 1970 to 1976, addressing the United Nations General Assembly in 1975

In choosing his successor, a president is governed by certain constitutional rules. The *tapado* must be Mexican-born of Mexican parents, male, at least thirty-five years old, and may not be a member of the clergy of any faith. Although he may adhere personally to a religious belief, the president along with other Government officials does not participate in his capacity as an officeholder in religious ceremonies or at church functions. In deciding on a president-designate, the chief executive may seek the advice and approval of PRI and other party leaders, governors and mayors of principal states and cities, former presidents, and representatives of peasant and worker organizations. But the final choice rests with him.

Often the *tapado* is a member of the cabinet, such as the minister of the interior. President López Portillo had held the post of minister of finance in the Echeverría cabinet since 1973. Whatever his background, the president-to-be does not disclose his views, even if they differ widely from those of the outgoing president, until after he has taken office on December 1 of the election year. The policies of the officeholder must be supported throughout his term. The candidate's campaign tour is largely a hand-shaking and getting-acquainted affair. And the posters and slogans that plaster Mexico for months in advance of the election are in part aimed at ensuring as high a voter turnout as possible when the day arrives. There is no vice-president. Should the chief executive die in office a provisional president is chosen by the congress and elected by the senate.

Interestingly, Mexico's presidents have not followed in the steps of their predecessors as closely as one might expect, possibly because each has sought to make his own name in the annals of Mexican history. Luis Echeverría Alvarez was believed to be as right-wing and conservative as President Gustavo Díaz Ordaz under whom he had served as minister of the interior. But once in office he boldly set forth a number of leftist views and policies, attacking Mexico's capitalists, distributing *ejido* lands to the peasantry, befriending the Communist leaders of Latin America (President Salvador Allende of Chile and Prime Minister Fidel Castro of Cuba), releasing some jailed students, and revoking the press censorship imposed by the Díaz Ordaz regime.

As his term in office progressed, however, it became evident that many ongoing abuses of civil rights were not going to be corrected and that the president's espousal of leftist causes was connected with his personal ambitions. On the international scene, Echeverría was anxious to put Mexico forward as a leader of the world's poorer countries and to promote himself as a spokesman for the developing nations of the third world. He called for a "new world economic order," whereby the gap between rich and poor countries would be narrowed. And he condemned the United States as a rich country that was trying to keep Mexico economically dependent upon it. Echeverría intended this stance to strengthen his bid for leadership in the United Nations. Although he failed in his attempt to win the post of Secretary General in 1976, he did move his country onto the world stage as no president before him had done.

At home, however, there was mounting criticism of Echeverría's costly travels to third-world countries. Many people felt that he was neglecting Mexico's economic problems and ignoring the implementation of social reforms, that while the president talked like a radical he behaved more like a conservative. Toward the close of his presidential term, Echeverría found Mexico's most prominent daily newspaper, *Excelsior*, in disagreement with some of his foreign-policy ideas. His response was to silence its opposition by removing its editor and some members of its staff. This act showed how fragile the freedoms of speech and of the press are in Mexico under the present system.

While the constitution of 1917 guarantees freedom of expression, it does set limits that open the way to censorship. The press and other media must respect private life, refrain from slanderous attacks, and take care not to disturb the peace, stir up public disorder, or incite to crime. Journalists have been jailed for their writings, but there are also subtler methods by which newspapers can be kept in line. Although presses are privately owned, the distribution of newsprint to newspapers and magazines is concentrated in the hands of a Government agency, so many editors are careful to follow a policy that will not be offensive to the Government. Other powerful groups also exercise control of the press. For example, a newspaper that criticizes the practices of big business may find itself subjected to an advertising boycott.

As the Government issues many news and information releases and advertises heavily in the press, the content of most dailies and weeklies is apt to reflect Government policies rather than independent viewpoints. Many newspapers even print publicity stories, for which they receive payment, but run them as legitimate news items rather than identifying them as the advertising and promotional material they really are. Sophisticated readers are cynical about the quality and reliability of most of the 200 dailies published in Mexico, primarily in Mexico City, Guadalajara, and Monterrey. The most popular magazines in Mexico are the Spanish-language version of the *Reader's Digest*; *Tiempo*, a news magazine modeled on *Time*; and *Buen Hogar*, a Spanish-language edition of *Good Housekeeping*.

Because of the country's rather high rate of illiteracy and its many small and scattered pockets of population, an overwhelming proportion of the Mexican public receives its news, information, and entertainment from radio rather than newspapers or magazines. Both

A grade-school classroom in an island village at Lake Pátzcuaro
reflecting Mexico's efforts to increase literacy
among its upcoming generation

radio and television broadcasting started late due to the problems of transmitting across mountainous terrain. The 1960's were the main period of development. Like the press, the broadcasting media are privately owned except for a few Government-subsidized educational stations on radio and television. These stations offer literacy courses and secondary-education classes for rural students who have no schooling available to them beyond the primary grades.

In addition to news and information programs, commercial radio brings soap operas, comedy skits, listener-request programs, and sporting events into Mexican homes. But the same strictures apply as to the press. News and other programs can be banned if deemed dangerous to the security of the state, a threat to public order and harmony, or an attack on individual honor, moral principles, or family life. Repeated abuses can lead to the Government's revoking broadcasters' licenses. The Government also airs its own programs on privately owned networks, presenting cultural events and news of Government activities. Much time—often twenty minutes out of every hour—is taken up with commercial messages on the private networks.

Television sets are, of course, too expensive for the average family to own. However, it has become a practice in poor city neighborhoods and even in some rural areas for a family to purchase a television set on credit and pay it off by charging admission to neighbors who view the programs on a regular basis. Among the most popular television programs are soap operas, variety shows, and dramatic and comedy series imported from the United States. Certain American crime shows, however, have been banned by Mexican authorities because of their violence and the possibility of their having a bad influence on youth.

Faced with the problems of how to ensure good taste, public order, and political stability, the Mexican Government does not flinch at the use of censorship throughout all branches of the mass media. This practice is strongly opposed by those in Mexico and elsewhere who maintain that real freedom of expression must be total freedom without limits or conditions.

Compared to the United States and some other Western democracies, Mexico's political structure is technically an authoritarian one and hence the state is more of a dictatorship than a democracy. It is also evident that the Mexican Government tends to use the tools of repression, particularly when challenged by ideas considered threatening to the "institutionalized revolution" that is so zealously guarded by the PRI.

Yet, to be fair, the system has operated with fewer violations of human rights than in the blatant dictatorships of the world. During the early months of the enlightened López Portillo presidency, over 400 political prisoners were freed, some unconditionally and others provisionally, and the Government declared that no persons charged with political crimes were being held in jail. The Mexican political system has also managed to maintain a relatively favorable climate for national development for a number of decades. The real danger of the system seems to lie in its potential. Under virtually one-party rule, the electorate is without true freedom of choice and lacks effective channels through which to voice its discontents. At the same time, the Government's executive, legislative, and judicial branches are without a framework of checks and balances. It does, therefore, seem conceivable that one day the suppression of freedoms in Mexico might escalate and the power centered in the presidency might spawn a ruthless, long-term dictatorship.

The swearing in of José López Portillo as president of Mexico on December 1, 1976, was viewed with favor and even with feelings of relief, both at home and abroad, for the Echeverría presidency had ended on a note of tension and discord. Within the country, the economy was deeply depressed, due in large part to Echeverría's massive public spending in an effort to prime the economy, raise workers' wages, and narrow the gap between rich and poor. At the same time, however, the outspoken president had driven out foreign

Middle-income housing projects such as this one
were included in President Echeverría's public-spending program

investment still badly needed in Mexico. He not only denounced
American-financed private enterprise, he tightened and strictly en-
forced Mexico's laws requiring all business operations to be at least
51 percent Mexican-owned. In some cases, Echeverría raised this
requirement to 60 and even 75 percent.

Conditions worsened in the final months of Echeverría's presidency when Mexico's currency had to be devalued. Since 1954, the
peso had remained at a stable rate of exchange of 12.5 to one United
States dollar. In view of Mexico's increasing economic difficulties,
this rate was unrealistically high. But after the Government ordered
devaluation, the peso dropped to roughly 25 to the dollar. As a
result, Mexicans had to pay twice as much for goods imported from

the United States. True, the Government's purpose had been to reduce foreign spending and keep pesos within the country, as well as to make Mexican exports cheaper and thus more attractive abroad. However, prices also began to rise within the country and inflation leaped to 30 percent during 1976. Nor did the country's export market show immediate growth.

Like other developing countries, Mexico had been particularly hard hit by the jump in world oil prices that had taken place in 1973. Not only did Mexican industry suffer by having to pay more for this vital commodity, the demand for Mexican raw materials was cut as other countries, too, began to feel the energy pinch. By 1974, much of the world had entered a period of economic recession. Mexico was soon afflicted by a severe balance-of-payments deficit: it was spending much more for imports than it was receiving for exports. As a result, the country was forced to borrow money from international banking sources, and by early 1977 Mexico ranked second only to Brazil as one of the world's largest debtor nations, owing some twenty-five billion dollars in foreign loans.

The Mexican economy is a mix of Government and private enterprise. Nearly one-quarter of the nation's business operations fall within the sector that is Government-owned and administered. Included are such basic industries as oil, petrochemicals, fertilizers, steel, railroads, aviation, electricity, and telecommunications. The Government has also invested in many mining operations and other private companies. Lest it appear, however, that Mexico has a socialist economy, it must be pointed out that private capitalist enterprises are strongly encouraged, particularly under the López Portillo administration, which seeks to win back the Mexican and foreign investors driven out under Echeverría.

Privately owned businesses provide Mexico with nearly all its consumer goods: processed foods, shoes, apparel, metal products, and other manufactured items. They also produce the nation's exports: minerals, coffee, sugar, cotton, sisal, tobacco, tomatoes, strawberries,

A large, privately owned farm growing cotton,
an important domestic and export crop for Mexico

chocolate, honey, tequila, chicle, timber, shrimp, and steel products.

A most important private industry for Mexico—responsible for nearly half the nation's foreign exchange—has been tourism, popularly known as *la industria sin chimeneas*, "the industry without chimneys." At some points during the early 1970's, tourism actually earned more for Mexico than the sum of its exports, with 80 to 90 percent of the visitors coming from the United States. But in late 1975 the influx of American tourists dropped sharply.

Once again the reason was related to President Echeverría's hostility toward the United States and his alliance with third-world causes. When African and Arab nations lined up in the United Nations to pass a resolution equating Zionism (the immigration policy of the Jewish state of Israel) with racism, Mexico joined in the vote condemning Israel, whose position was supported by the United States. Immediately a number of Jewish organizations in the

United States that had been arranging a heavy schedule of travel programs to Mexico instituted a boycott of that country. Other would-be American tourists also canceled their reservations because they considered the Mexican vote anti-American.

The loss in income from tourism that prevailed throughout 1976 posed another serious economic problem for the new López Portillo administration. Although the boycott was gradually withdrawn after the president took office, lingering bad publicity, plus reports of incidents of banditry and fears of domestic unrest, prevented a quick resurgence of the tourist trade. Yet Mexican authorities hoped that the attractions of the devalued peso and of the new resorts built with the aid of a special Government trust fund would lure Americans back to their country's sunny beaches, dramatic ruins, and picturesque colonial towns. Among the newest water-sports resorts were those built at Cancún on the Yucatán, on the island of Cozumel off its coast, along the Pacific shore in line with the older holiday spots of Acapulco and Puerto Vallarta, and on Baja California.

Another hope for improvement in the Mexican economy lies in the growth of Mexico's oil-exporting capability. Some estimates of the country's total (unproven) reserves, made by American companies, are as high as sixty billion barrels, six times greater than the estimated reserves of Alaska's North Slope. If this figure is accurate and if Mexico can secure the funds to extract and market its oil, it is possible that the country could become an oil exporter comparable to Venezuela by the late 1980's.

However, there are many stumbling blocks. Not only is the cost of getting the oil out of the ground and from offshore sources enormous, but Mexican laws prohibit international oil companies from acquiring a stake in Mexican reserves. All exploration and drilling would have to be done either by PEMEX (Petroleos Mexicanos, the state-owned monopoly) or by foreign companies on a straight service-contract basis. The same would apply to the building of the recently proposed 800-mile natural-gas pipeline to run along the Gulf Coast from the state of Tabasco into Texas, to supply the United States market.

As foreign companies are unlikely to offer financial aid without a sharing in the wealth, the Mexican Government would have to undertake heavy foreign borrowing, on top of its already huge foreign debt. But Mexico is proud of the nationalization of its oil industry, by President Cárdenas in 1938, and it is still on its guard against the kind of foreign economic exploitation that flourished during the Porfirio Díaz regime.

Nor does Mexico plan to sell its oil and gas at bargain prices. Although not a member of OPEC (Organization of Petroleum Exporting Countries) as of late 1977, Mexico has gone along with the world cartel and raised its prices in line with theirs. The United States is almost certain to be Mexico's biggest crude-oil and natural-gas customer as production increases. At the same time, Mexico expects to double its refining capacity and thus become self-sufficient in its domestic oil needs.

Still another effort to improve the economy was made in 1976 when the Mexican Government established a 200-mile zone of restricted fishing off its eastern and western coasts. Among the steps taken to conserve Mexico's sea resources and to increase its revenues were new limitations on sport fishing in the 600-mile-long Gulf of California and the imposition of higher tariffs on foreign fishing vessels. Eventually, through a resurgence of tourism and a profitable yield from its oil, natural gas, and sea resources, Mexico hopes to relieve its depressed economy and soaring foreign indebtedness.

The current basic difficulty with the Mexican economic situation is one that afflicts many other developing nations. New jobs cannot be generated while as much as half the population remains outside the market economy. Poor rural and urban families use very few factory-made products of the type that require large labor contingents. Such families cannot afford to buy washing machines or

Life tends to stagnate in Mexico's tiny communities
where participation in the national economy is minimal

television sets or automobiles. They live in houses made of natural
or even waste materials, make most of their own clothing, and grow
most of their own food. Nor do they have the opportunity to raise
their standard of living and begin to interact with the economy at
large. One means of advancement would be through well-paid jobs
in industry, the very jobs that are so sharply limited. So the Mexican
economy, like the average peasant or poor urban dweller, tends to
stagnate.

An organized labor movement does exist in Mexico, but, like the
country's social-security system, the labor unions are of benefit only
to those who work at regular and substantial jobs. They do not represent those in marginal occupations. The one-third of the work
force that is unemployed, plus the many underemployed, are un-

protected by unions such as the large Confederación de Trabaja-dores Mexicanos (CTM), or Mexican Workers' Federation. Although the CTM claims a membership of two million, a number of splinter groups have left the federation because they have felt that the strides won by its union leadership have been at the worker's ex-pense. The CTM has been willing to cooperate closely with the Government and to share its gains with the much-favored private-enterprise sector. Many laborers feel that private enterprise has benefited more from the Revolution than has the worker.

Mexico's agricultural economy is divided between the large mechanized and irrigated farms and the small peasant and *ejido* operations, and the disparity between the two is very great. Half the country's total agricultural product is provided by modern farming estates, although these comprise only 4 percent of the total number of farms; a mere 1 percent of such farms raises all of Mexico's considerable agricultural exports.

In sharp contrast to these successful commercial farms are the plots of the small, impoverished farmers who still plow with oxen, harvest by hand, make do without fertilizers, and can only hope for rain in a climate that is prone to drought. The efficiency of their operation is minimal, and the productivity of their land is under-standably low. Although nearly half the country's cropland is still given over to the growing of corn, even that staple food has had to be imported in recent years. The same is true for wheat. Mexico's success with new high-yield strains of wheat, introduced in 1966, was soon offset by population growth and increased demand for wheat-flour products, especially among the growing middle class.

Self-sufficiency in rice, beans, sugar, coffee, cotton, fruits and vegetables, livestock and fish was still being maintained in the late 1970's. But Mexico's rapidly growing population poses a serious threat to their continued adequacy. Even if crop production were to become greatly intensified throughout the agricultural sector (which appears highly unlikely), it seems clear that industrial production, too, must be stepped up. Only in this way can Mexico assure the well-being of coming generations and, at the same time, see the Mexican economy develop. Soon after taking office, President López Portillo expressed this goal in calling for "an industrial-agricultural alliance for production."

There are a number of factors favoring improvement of Mexico's economic status. Among them are the country's long-term political stability, its wide range of natural resources, and its proximity to the United States, which is both a market for its exports and a source of tourists. At present, over 55 percent of Mexico's exports go to the United States. But Mexicans would like to see an increase, more in keeping with the over 60 percent of imports that come from the United States. Principal among these are machinery, motor vehicles, and chemicals. A particularly sore point with Mexicans is United States protectionism, which limits the import of some Mexican agricultural and manufactured products—among them shoes—in order to keep down competition with American goods and products.

Plowing a field with oxen in age-old fashion

The United States on Mexican minds:
an American Bicentennial exhibit
in Mexico City's Chapultepec Park

José López Portillo began his presidency in a much friendlier spirit toward the United States than had been shown by his predecessor. While he upheld Mexico's right of alignment with the poorer nations of the world, he avowed no aspirations toward third-world leadership. On the sensitive issue of the illegal immigration of Mexicans into the United States, López Portillo maintained that this situation was a direct outgrowth of Mexico's economic problems, problems that could be alleviated by the United States allowing more Mexican imports into the country. Jobs would thus be created through "trade, not aid" and would keep many would-be Mexican migrants at home. On the other hand, it seemed clear that should American business interests protest a rise in Mexican imports, the United States would probably have little choice but to continue to serve as a safety valve for Mexico's explosive, poverty-ridden population.

There is an old Mexican saying: "So far from God, so close to the

A memento of the Good Neighbor era:
a plaque bearing Mexico's coat of arms
on New York City's Avenue of the Americas

United States." And indeed it is probably true that Mexico focuses
on its neighbor across the border much more intensely than the
United States does on Mexico. Yet there is no question that the
two countries are highly interdependent. Mexico is its northern
neighbor's fourth largest customer, and the United States is Mexico's
biggest foreign investor and creditor. It is in the interest of the
United States to avert any catastrophic changes in the Mexican
system, political or otherwise. Whatever happens on the other side
of the 2000-mile, difficult-to-defend border—sometimes described
as the "soft underbelly" of the United States—is bound to create
strong reverberations to the north.

Mexicans have many legitimate grievances against their powerful
neighbor. They have not forgotten that over a century ago the
United States involved them in a war that stripped Mexico of nearly
half its territory, or that it has several times invaded their country.
Episodes occurred as recently as 1914, when American forces occu-

pied Veracruz, and again in 1916, when General John J. Pershing drove deep into Mexico in pursuit of Pancho Villa. Mexicans have not forgotten that American enterprises reaped enormous profits from Mexico's natural resources during the *porfiriato*. And they are all too aware that the Pan American Good Neighbor Policy, proclaimed by President Franklin D. Roosevelt in 1933, was motivated in part by the threat of Fascist takeovers and impending war in Europe.

Today Mexicans feel that Americans hold them unduly responsible for the drug traffic that flourishes in the United States, and they know how much Americans resent the inflow of illegal migrant laborers. Perhaps the Americans' treatment of Indians and blacks

The railroad station at Nogales, a Mexican town on the Arizona border where legal entrants into the United States may be processed

contribute to the Mexicans' unease also. Nonetheless, Mexicans have a genuine admiration for their wealthy and progressive North American neighbor. Most view the term of President López Portillo as opening a new era of understanding and cooperation between the two countries, one far less tainted with bitterness and mistrust than in the past.

As the geographical gateway to Latin America, Mexico shares many features, particularly aspects of its cultural heritage, with that part of the world. But its allegiances in recent decades have been based mainly on ideological sympathies and have once again brought it into an area of conflict with the United States. As a member of the Organization of American States (which was established at the Pan American Conference of 1948), Mexico was the only country to vote against the ousting of Cuba, in 1962, because of its Communist government. Mexico denounced the American attempt to invade Cuba, in 1961, during President John F. Kennedy's administration. And even after the island nation's expulsion from the OAS, Mexico refused to suspend diplomatic and economic relations with Cuba and encouraged other members of the OAS to restore such relations.

The Mexican Government was outraged by the 1973 overthrow and death of Chile's Communist leader, President Salvador Allende. The coup was alleged to have involved United States complicity. Mexico severed diplomatic relations with Chile's new right-wing regime in 1974 because of its brutal violations of human rights. In another area that is touchy, Mexico supports full and immediate Panamanian sovereignty over the American-built Panama Canal rather than even gradual relinquishment of United States control.

Latin America is Mexico's second largest trading partner after the United States, and some of its southern neighbors, particularly the small bordering states of Central America that were once part of New Spain, actually regard Mexico as another "colossus of the North," almost as threatening to them economically as the

United States has often appeared to Mexico. As Mexico has imported technology from the United States and other industrialized nations, it has developed a kind of know-how that is now becoming exportable to Latin America. Processes such as steel reduction, oil refining, and the production of paper from sugarcane residue have all been adopted, through Mexican experience, to the needs of less developed nations. Thus Mexico is beginning to serve as a filterer of highly sophisticated technologies to other American, as well as some African and Asian, countries and to earn a reputation for its industrial expertise.

To the consternation of some of the right-wing dictatorships of South America—particularly those of Chile, Argentina, and Uruguay —Mexico has offered itself as a haven for political exiles, many of whom are leftists. The Government has provided living quarters and other assistance for those refugees who are in need. Although opportunities for work are limited in Mexico, even for those newcomers with professional backgrounds, most prefer it to exile in Europe or elsewhere because of the Spanish language and familiar cultural patterns, and because of the camaraderie of other countrymen and broad news coverage of events at home.

While Mexico is by no means a leftist state, the tradition of giving asylum to political refugees of liberal and left-wing persuasion has strong roots in the Spanish Civil War, which took place from 1936 to 1939. During that period, President Lázaro Cárdenas welcomed many Spanish Republican refugees to Mexico, and, after the Fascist regime of Generalissimo Francisco Franco was established in Spain, a Spanish government-in-exile was set up in Mexico City. Franco died in 1975. In the early part of 1977, after thirty-eight years during which Mexico had no relations with its former mother country, diplomatic ties between the two were resumed.

As with the United States, Mexico has had a long-term love-hate relationship with Spain: The culture of that country is deeply ingrained in Mexican life and almost every Mexican has the blood of the Spanish conquerors flowing in his veins. At the same time, the mestizo's heritage is also that of the Indian defeated and used by the Spaniard.

Elsewhere on the international scene, Mexico has trading relations with Japan, its third largest economic partner. Canada and western Europe rank next in foreign trade volume. In the area of diplomatic relations, there is a void between Mexico and the Vatican due to the Mexican Government's long years of conflict with the Roman Catholic church inside the country. Yet, although no official relations exist, President Echeverría did visit the Pope in 1974 in the course of his world travels.

Mexico severed diplomatic relations with the Soviet Union in 1930 and, in 1937, gave political asylum to Leon Trotsky, the ousted Bolshevik leader. In 1940, Trotsky was assassinated in Mexico City by a secret-police agent of his enemy, Soviet leader Joseph Stalin. Relations between the two nations were resumed in 1942, but have remained merely cordial. Mexico's stance in defense of Cuba (which has been strongly influenced and supported by the Soviet Union) may well be an anti-American pose through which Mexico seeks to express its own nonalignment rather than a pro-Soviet position.

Mexico's trade with eastern Europe is quite small. The same is true of its trade with the third world, largely because the raw materials and other products of those countries are similar to and, therefore, competitive with those of Mexico rather than complementary. Mexico enjoys a lively cultural interaction with many countries, however, because of the interest of archeologists and other international scholars in its rich Indian origins.

Today's Mexico is a nation still in the process of becoming. Socially, politically, and economically it is foundering in the gap between the still-distant dream of the Revolution of 1910 and the reality of the present. President López Portillo seemed deeply aware of that reality when he spoke early in 1977 (before the United States House of Representatives) of Mexico's need to supply its people with "equal security . . . against such elemental risks of life as hunger, disease, ignorance, and helplessness" before it could guarantee equal opportunities.

In the decades since the dream of 1910 was institutionalized, Mexico, like other developing nations, has also found itself grappling less than successfully with problems imposed by the world outside its borders—problems of technology, trade, financing, and high energy costs. International solutions will most likely be required,

A Mexican farm woman for whom the promises of the Revolution will probably not be realized

A child who may yet see the day
when reality will draw closer to the Mexican dream

and Mexico looks, above all, to the United States for the tools of
self-help.

As author of a mystical novel published in 1965 about the god,
Quetzalcoatl, López Portillo wrote: "The star we live on follows
a regular course; but the men who live on it form their behavior in
an arbitrary way." Despite the obstacles in its course, Mexico is
patiently committed to the goal of fulfillment. Looking back, the
long stony centuries stretch away deep into time; looking ahead,
the day may well be comparatively close at hand when the reality
will draw closer to the dream.

Bibliography

Bushnell, G. H. S. *The First Americans: The Pre-Columbian Civilizations.*
New York: McGraw-Hill Book Company, 1968.

Crow, John A. *Mexico Today.* New York: Harper & Row, 1972.

Diaz, May N. *Tonalá; Conservatism, Responsibility, & Authority in a Mexican Town.* Berkeley: University of California Press, 1966.

Ewing, Russell C., ed. *Six Faces of Mexico.* Tucson: University of Arizona Press, 1966.

Lewis, Oscar. *Five Families; Mexican Case Studies in the Culture of Poverty.* New York: Basic Books, 1959.

Lewis, Oscar. *The Children of Sánchez; Autobiography of a Mexican Family.* New York: Random House, 1961.

López-Portillo y Pacheco, José. *Quetzalcoatl.* Translated by Eliot Weinberger and Diana S. Goodrich. New York: Seabury Press, 1976.

Weil, Thomas E., and others. *Area Handbook for Mexico.* Washington, D.C.: U.S. Government Printing Office, 1975.

Index

Lila Perl was born and educated in New York City, and she holds a B.A. degree from Brooklyn College. In addition, she has taken graduate work at Teachers College, Columbia University, and at the School of Education, New York University. She is the author of a number of books for adults and for children, both fiction and non-fiction. Several of them concern life in other lands. In preparation for writing these, Miss Perl travels extensively in the country, doing firsthand research and taking many photographs. Her husband, Charles Yerkow, is also a writer, and they live in Beechhurst, New York.

This book may be kept

FOURTEEN DAYS

A fine will be charged for each day the book is kept overtime.

GAYLORD 142			PRINTED IN U.S.A.